English Men of Letters

EDITED BY JOHN MORLEY

SAMUEL JOHNSON

SAMUEL JOHNSON

BY

LESLIE STEPHEN

AMS PRESS
NEW YORK

Reprinted from the edition of 1887, London
First AMS EDITION published 1968
Manufactured in the United States of America

Library of Congress Catalogue Card Number: 68-58398

AMS PRESS, INC.
New York, N.Y. 10003

CONTENTS.

SAMUEL JOHNSON

SAMUEL JOHNSON.

CHAPTER I.

CHILDHOOD AND EARLY LIFE.

SAMUEL JOHNSON was born in Lichfield in 1709. His father, Michael Johnson, was a bookseller, highly respected by the cathedral clergy, and for a time sufficiently prosperous to be a magistrate of the town, and, in the year of his son's birth, sheriff of the county. He opened a bookstall on market-days at neighbouring towns, including Birmingham, which was as yet unable to maintain a separate bookseller. The tradesman often exaggerates the prejudices of the class whose wants he supplies, and Michael Johnson was probably a more devoted High Churchman and Tory than many of the cathedral clergy themselves. He reconciled himself with difficulty to taking the oaths against the exiled dynasty. He was a man of considerable mental and physical power, but tormented by hypochondriacal tendencies. His son inherited a share both of his constitution and of his principles. Long afterwards Samuel associated with his childish days a faint but solemn recollection of a lady in diamonds and long black hood. The lady

B

was Queen Anne, to whom, in compliance with a superstition just dying a natural death, he had been taken by
his mother to be touched for the king's evil. The touch
was ineffectual. Perhaps, as Boswell suggested, he ought to
have been presented to the genuine heirs of the Stuarts in
Rome. Disease and superstition had thus stood by his
cradle, and they never quitted him during life. The de-
mon of hypochondria was always lying in wait for him,
and could be exorcised for a time only by hard work or
social excitement. Of this we shall hear enough; but it
may be as well to sum up at once some of the physical
characteristics which marked him through life and greatly
influenced his career.

The disease had scarred and disfigured features otherwise regular and always impressive. It had seriously
injured his eyes, entirely destroying, it seems, the sight of
one. He could not, it is said, distinguish a friend's face
half a yard off, and pictures were to him meaningless
patches, in which he could never see the resemblance to
their objects. The statement is perhaps exaggerated; for
he could see enough to condemn a portrait of himself.
He expressed some annoyance when Reynolds had painted
him with a pen held close to his eye; and protested that
he would not be handed down to posterity as "blinking
Sam." It seems that habits of minute attention atoned in
some degree for this natural defect. Boswell tells us how
Johnson once corrected him as to the precise shape of a
mountain; and Mrs. Thrale says that he was a close and
exacting critic of ladies' dress, even to the accidental
position of a riband. He could even lay down æsthetical
canons upon such matters. He reproved her for wearing
a dark dress as unsuitable to a "little creature." "What,"
he asked, "have not all insects gay colours?" His insen-

sibility to music was even more pronounced than his dulness of sight. On hearing it said, in praise of a musical performance, that it was in any case difficult, his feeling comment was, "I wish it had been impossible!"

The queer convulsions by which he amazed all beholders were probably connected with his disease, though he and Reynolds ascribed them simply to habit. When entering a doorway with his blind companion, Miss Williams, he would suddenly desert her on the step in order to "whirl and twist about" in strange gesticulations. The performance partook of the nature of a superstitious ceremonial. He would stop in a street or the middle of a room to go through it correctly. Once he collected a laughing mob in Twickenham meadows by his antics; his hands imitating the motions of a jockey riding at full speed and his feet twisting in and out to make heels and toes touch alternately. He presently sat down and took out a *Grotius De Veritate*, over which he "seesawed" so violently that the mob ran back to see what was the matter. Once in such a fit he suddenly twisted off the shoe of a lady who sat by him. Sometimes he seemed to be obeying some hidden impulse, which commanded him to touch every post in a street or tread on the centre of every paving-stone, and would return if his task had not been accurately performed.

In spite of such oddities, he was not only possessed of physical power corresponding to his great height and massive stature, but was something of a proficient at athletic exercises. He was conversant with the theory, at least, of boxing; a knowledge probably acquired from an uncle who kept the ring at Smithfield for a year, and was never beaten in boxing or wrestling. His constitutional fearlessness would have made him a formidable antagonist.

Hawkins describes the oak staff, six feet in length and increasing from one to three inches in diameter, which lay ready to his hand when he expected an attack from Macpherson of Ossian celebrity. Once he is said to have taken up a chair at the theatre upon which a man had seated himself during his temporary absence, and to have tossed it and its occupant bodily into the pit. He would swim into pools said to be dangerous, beat huge dogs into peace, climb trees, and even run races and jump gates. Once at least he went out foxhunting, and though he despised the amusement, was deeply touched by the complimentary assertion that he rode as well as the most illiterate fellow in England. Perhaps the most whimsical of his performances was when, in his fifty-fifth year, he went to the top of a high hill with his friend Langton. "I have not had a roll for a long time," said the great lexicographer suddenly, and, after deliberately emptying his pockets, he laid himself parallel to the edge of the hill, and descended, turning over and over till he came to the bottom. We may believe, as Mrs. Thrale remarks upon his jumping over a stool to show that he was not tired by his hunting, that his performances in this kind were so strange and uncouth that a fear for the safety of his bones quenched the spectator's tendency to laugh.

In such a strange case was imprisoned one of the most vigorous intellects of the time. Vast strength hampered by clumsiness and associated with grievous disease, deep and massive powers of feeling limited by narrow though acute perceptions, were characteristic both of soul and body. These peculiarities were manifested from his early infancy. Miss Seward, a typical specimen of the provincial *précieuse*, attempted to trace them in an epitaph which he was said to have written at the age of three.

Here lies good master duck
Whom Samuel Johnson trod on ;
If it had lived, it had been good luck,
For then we had had an odd one.

The verses, however, were really made by his father, who passed them off as the child's, and illustrate nothing but the paternal vanity. In fact the boy was regarded as something of an infant prodigy. His great powers of memory, characteristic of a mind singularly retentive of all impressions, were early developed. He seemed to learn by intuition. Indolence, as in his after life, alternated with brief efforts of strenuous exertion. His want of sight prevented him from sharing in the ordinary childish sports ; and one of his great pleasures was in reading old romances —a taste which he retained through life. Boys of this temperament are generally despised by their fellows ; but Johnson seems to have had the power of enforcing the respect of his companions. Three of the lads used to come for him in the morning and carry him in triumph to school, seated upon the shoulders of one and supported on each side by his companions.

After learning to read at a dame-school, and from a certain Tom Brown, of whom it is only recorded that he published a spelling-book and dedicated it to the Universe, young Samuel was sent to the Lichfield Grammar School, and was afterwards, for a short time, apparently in the character of pupil-teacher, at the school of Stourbridge, in Worcestershire. A good deal of Latin was " whipped into him," and though he complained of the excessive severity of two of his teachers, he was always a believer in the virtues of the rod. A child, he said, who is flogged, " gets his task, and there's an end on't ; whereas by exciting emulation and comparisons of superiority, you lay the foundations of lasting mischief; you make brothers and sisters hate each other." In practice, indeed, this stern disciplinarian seems to have been specially indulgent to children. The memory of his own sorrows made him value their happiness, and he rejoiced greatly when he at last persuaded a schoolmaster to remit the old-fashioned holiday-task.

Johnson left school at sixteen and spent two years at home, probably in learning his father's business. This seems to have been the chief period of his studies. Long afterwards he said that he knew almost as much at eighteen as he did at the age of fifty-three—the date of the remark. His father's shop would give him many opportunities, and he devoured what came in his way with the undiscriminating eagerness of a young student. His intellectual resembled his physical appetite. He gorged books. He tore the hearts out of them, but did not study systematically. Do you read books through? he asked indignantly of some one who expected from him such supererogatory labour. His memory enabled him to accumulate great stores of a desultory and unsystematic knowledge. Somehow he became a fine Latin scholar, though never first-rate as a Grecian. The direction of his studies was partly determined by the discovery of a folio of Petrarch, lying on a shelf where he was looking for apples; and one of his earliest literary plans, never carried out, was an edition of Politian, with a history of Latin poetry from the time of Petrarch. When he went to the University at the end of this period, he was in possession of a very unusual amount of reading.

Meanwhile he was beginning to feel the pressure of poverty. His father's affairs were probably getting into disorder. One anecdote—it is one which it is difficult to read without emotion—refers to this period. Many years afterwards, Johnson, worn by disease and the hard struggle of life, was staying at Lichfield, where a few old friends still survived, but in which every street must have revived the memories of the many who had long since gone over to the majority. He was missed one morning at breakfast, and did not return till supper-time. Then he told how his time had been passed. On that day fifty years before, his father, confined by illness, had begged him to take his place to sell books at a stall at Uttoxeter. Pride made him refuse. " To do away with the sin of this dis-obedience, I this day went in a post-chaise to Uttoxeter, and going into the market at the time of high business, uncovered my head and stood with it bare an hour before the stall which my father had formerly used, exposed to the sneers of the standers-by and the inclemency of the weather; a penance by which I trust I have propitiated Heaven for this only instance, I believe, of contumacy to my father." If the anecdote illustrates the touch of superstition in Johnson's mind, it reveals too that sacred depth of tenderness which ennobled his character. No repentance can ever wipe out the past or make it be as though it had not been; but the remorse of a fine cha-racter may be transmuted into a permanent source of nobler views of life and the world.

There are difficulties in determining the circumstances and duration of Johnson's stay at Oxford. He began residence at Pembroke College in 1728. It seems pro-bable that he received some assistance from a gentle-man whose son took him as companion, and from the clergy of Lichfield, to whom his father was known, and who were aware of the son's talents. Possibly his college assisted him during part of the time. It is certain that he left without taking a degree, though he probably resided for nearly three years. It is certain, also, that his father's bankruptcy made his stay difficult, and that the period must have been one of trial.

The effect of the Oxford residence upon Johnson's mind was characteristic. The lad already suffered from the attacks of melancholy, which sometimes drove him to the borders of insanity. At Oxford, Law's *Serious Call* gave him the strong religious impressions which remained through life. But he does not seem to have been regarded as a gloomy or a religious youth by his contemporaries. When told in after years that he had been described as a " gay and frolicsome fellow," he replied, " Ah! sir, I was mad and violent. It was bitterness which they mistook for frolic. I was miserably poor, and I thought to fight my way by my literature and my wit; so I disregarded all power and all authority." Though a hearty supporter of authority in principle, Johnson was distinguished through life by the strongest spirit of personal independence and self-respect. He held, too, the sound doctrine, deplored by his respectable biographer Hawkins, that the scholar's life, like the Christian's, levelled all distinctions of rank. When an officious benefactor put a pair of new shoes at his door, he threw them away with indignation. He seems to have treated his tutors with a contempt which Boswell politely attributed to "great fortitude of mind," but Johnson himself set down as "stark insensibility." The life of a poor student is not, one may fear, even yet exempt from much bitterness, and in those days the position was far more servile than at present. The servitors and sizars had much to bear from richer companions. A proud melancholy lad, conscious of great powers, had to meet with hard rebuffs, and tried to meet them by returning scorn for scorn.

Such distresses, however, did not shake Johnson's rooted Toryism. He fully imbibed, if he did not already share, the strongest prejudices of the place, and his misery never produced a revolt against the system, though it may have fostered insolence to individuals. Three of the most eminent men with whom Johnson came in contact in later life, had also been students at Oxford. Wesley, his senior by six years, was a fellow of Lincoln whilst Johnson was an undergraduate, and was learning at Oxford the necessity of rousing his countrymen from the religious lethargy into which they had sunk. " Have not pride and haughtiness of spirit, impatience, and peevishness, sloth and indolence, gluttony and sensuality, and even a proverbial uselessness been objected to us, perhaps not always by our enemies nor wholly without ground ? " So said Wesley, preaching before the University of Oxford in 1744, and the words in his mouth imply more than the preacher's formality. Adam Smith, Johnson's junior by fourteen years, was so impressed by the utter indifference of Oxford authorities to their duties, as to find in it an admirable illustration of the consequences of the neglect of the true principles of supply and demand implied in the endowment of learning. Gibbon, his junior by twenty-eight years, passed at Oxford the " most idle and unprofitable " months of his whole life ; and was, he said, as willing to disclaim the university for a mother, as she could be to renounce him for a son. Oxford, as judged by these men, was remarkable as an illustration of the spiritual and intellectual decadence of a body which at other times has been a centre of great movements of thought. Johnson, though he had a rougher experience than any of the three, loved Oxford as though she had not been a harsh step-mother to his youth. Sir, he said fondly of his college, " we are a nest of singing-birds." Most of the strains are now pretty well forgotten, and some of them must at all times have been such as we scarcely associate with the nightingale. Johnson, however, cherished his college friendships, delighted in paying visits to his old university, and was deeply touched by the academical honours by which Oxford long afterwards recognized an eminence scarcely fostered by its protection. Far from sharing the doctrines of Adam Smith, he only regretted that the universities were not richer, and expressed a desire which will be understood by advocates of the " endowment of research," that there were many places of a thousand a year at Oxford.

On leaving the University, in 1731, the world was all before him. His father died in the end of the year, and Johnson's whole immediate inheritance was twenty pounds. Where was he to turn for daily bread? Even in those days, most gates were barred with gold and opened but to golden keys. The greatest chance for a poor man was probably through the Church. The career of Warburton, who rose from a similar position to a bishopric might have been rivalled by Johnson, and his connexions with Lichfield might, one would suppose, have helped him to a start. It would be easy to speculate upon causes which might have hindered such a career. In later life, he more than once refused to take orders upon the promise of a living. Johnson, as we know him, was a man of the world; though a religious man of the world. He represents the secular rather than the ecclesiastical type. So far as his mode of teaching goes, he is rather a disciple of Socrates than of St. Paul or Wesley. According to

him, a " tavern-chair " was " the throne of human felicity,"
and supplied a better arena than the pulpit for the utterance
of his message to mankind. And, though his external
circumstances doubtless determined his method, there was
much in his character which made it congenial. Johnson's
religious emotions were such as to make habitual reserve
almost a sanitary necessity. They were deeply coloured
by his constitutional melancholy. Fears of death and hell
were prominent in his personal creed. To trade upon his
feelings like a charlatan would have been abhorrent to his
masculine character ; and to give them full and frequent
utterance like a genuine teacher of mankind would have
been to imperil his sanity. If he had gone through the
excitement of a Methodist conversion, he would probably
have ended his days in a madhouse.

Such considerations, however, were not, one may guess,
distinctly present to Johnson himself; and the offer of a
college fellowship or of private patronage might probably
have altered his career. He might have become a learned
recluse or a struggling Parson Adams. College fellowships
were less open to talent then than now, and patrons were
never too propitious to the uncouth giant, who had to force
his way by sheer labour, and fight for his own hand. Accordingly, the young scholar tried to coin his brains into
money by the most depressing and least hopeful of employ-
ments. By becoming an usher in a school, he could at least
turn his talents to account with little delay, and that was
the most pressing consideration. By one schoolmaster he
was rejected on the ground that his infirmities would excite
the ridicule of the boys. Under another he passed some
months of " complicated misery," and could never think
of the school without horror and aversion. Finding this
situation intolerable, he settled in Birmingham, in 1733,

to be near an old schoolfellow, named Hector, who was
apparently beginning to practise as a surgeon.   Johnson
seems to have had some acquaintances among the comfortable families in the neighbourhood ; but his means of
living are obscure.   Some small literary work came in his
way.   He contributed essays to a local paper, and translated
a book of Travels in Abyssinia.   For this, his first publication, he received five guineas.   In 1734 he made certain
overtures to Cave, a London publisher, of the result of
which I shall have to speak presently.   For the present it
is pretty clear that the great problem of self-support had
been very inadequately solved.

Having no money and no prospects, Johnson naturally
married.   The attractions of the lady were not very
manifest to others than her husband.   She was the
widow of a Birmingham mercer named Porter.   Her age
at the time (1735) of the second marriage was forty-six,
the bridegroom being not quite twenty-six.   The biographer's eye was not fixed upon Johnson till after his
wife's death, and we have little in the way of authentic
description of her person and character.   Garrick, who
had known her, said that she was very fat, with cheeks
coloured both by paint and cordials, flimsy and fantastic
in dress and affected in her manners.   She is said to have
treated her husband with some contempt, adopting the
airs of an antiquated beauty, which he returned by
elaborate deference.   Garrick used his wonderful powers
of mimicry to make fun of the uncouth caresses of the
husband, and the courtly Beauclerc used to provoke the
smiles of his audience by repeating Johnson's assertion
that "it was a love-match on both sides."   One incident
of the wedding-day was ominous.   As the newly-married
couple rode back from church, Mrs. Johnson showed her

spirit by reproaching her husband for riding too fast, and then for lagging behind. Resolved " not to be made the slave of caprice," he pushed on briskly till he was fairly out of sight. When she rejoined him, as he, of course, took care that she should soon do, she was in tears. Mrs. Johnson apparently knew how to regain supremacy ; but, at any rate, Johnson loved her devotedly during life, and clung to her memory during a widowhood of more than thirty years, as fondly as if they had been the most pattern hero and heroine of romantic fiction.

Whatever Mrs. Johnson's charms, she seems to have been a woman of good sense and some literary judgment. Johnson's grotesque appearance did not prevent her from saying to her daughter on their first introduction, " This is the most sensible man I ever met." Her praises were, we may believe, sweeter to him than those of the severest critics, or the most fervent of personal flatterers. Like all good men, Johnson loved good women, and liked to have on hand a flirtation or two, as warm as might be within the bounds of due decorum. But nothing affected his fidelity to his Tetty or displaced her image in his mind. He remembered her in many solemn prayers, and such words as " this was dear Tetty's book :" or, " this was a prayer which dear Tetty was accustomed to say," were found written by him in many of her books of devotion.

Mrs. Johnson had one other recommendation—a fortune, namely, of £800—little enough, even then, as a provision for the support of the married pair, but enough to help Johnson to make a fresh start. In 1736, there appeared an advertisement in the *Gentleman's Magazine*. " At Edial, near Lichfield, in Staffordshire, young gentlemen are boarded and taught the Latin and Greek languages by Samuel Johnson." If, as seems probable, Mrs. Johnson's money supplied the funds for this venture, it was an unlucky speculation.

Johnson was not fitted to be a pedagogue. Success in that profession implies skill in the management of pupils, but perhaps still more decidedly in the management of parents. Johnson had little qualifications in either way. As a teacher he would probably have been alternately despotic and over-indulgent; and, on the other hand, a single glance at the rough Dominie Sampson would be enough to frighten the ordinary parent off his premises. Very few pupils came, and they seem to have profited little, if a story as told of two of his pupils refers to this time. After some months of instruction in English history, he asked them who had destroyed the monasteries? One of them gave no answer; the other replied "Jesus Christ." Johnson, however, could boast of one eminent pupil in David Garrick, though, by Garrick's account, his master was of little service except as affording an excellent mark for his early powers of ridicule. The school, or "academy," failed after a year and a half; and Johnson, once more at a loss for employment, resolved to try the great experiment, made so often and so often unsuccessfully. He left Lichfield to seek his fortune in London. Garrick accompanied him, and the two brought a common letter of introduction to the master of an academy from Gilbert Walmsley, registrar of the Prerogative Court in Lichfield. Long afterwards Johnson took an opportunity in the *Lives of the Poets*, of expressing his warm regard for the memory of his early friend, to whom he had been recommended by a community of literary tastes, in spite of party differences and great inequality of age. Walmsley says in his letter, that "one Johnson" is about to accompany Garrick to London, in order to try his fate with a tragedy and get himself employed in translation. Johnson, he adds, " is a very good scholar and poet, and I have great hopes will turn out a fine tragedy writer."

The letter is dated March 2nd, 1737. Before recording what is known of his early career thus started, it will be well to take a glance at the general condition of the profession of Literature in England at this period.

CHAPTER II.

LITERARY CAREER.

" No man but a blockhead," said Johnson, "ever wrote except for money." The doctrine is, of course, perfectly outrageous, and specially calculated to shock people who like to keep it for their private use, instead of proclaiming it in public. But it is a good expression of that huge contempt for the foppery of high-flown sentiment which, as is not uncommon with Johnson, passes into something which would be cynical if it were not half-humorous. In this case it implies also the contempt of the professional for the amateur. Johnson despised gentlemen who dabbled in his craft, as a man whose life is devoted to music or painting despises the ladies and gentlemen who treat those arts as fashionable accomplishments. An author was, according to him, a man who turned out books as a bricklayer turns out houses or a tailor coats. So long as he supplied a good article and got a fair price, he was a fool to grumble, and a humbug to affect loftier motives.

Johnson was not the first professional author, in this sense, but perhaps the first man who made the profession respectable. The principal habitat of authors, in his age, was Grub Street—a region which, in later years, has ceased to be ashamed of itself, and has adopted the more pretentious name Bohemia. The original Grub Street, it is said, first became associated with authorship during the increase of pamphlet literature, produced by the civil wars. Fox, the martyrologist, was one of its original inhabitants. Another of its heroes was a certain Mr. Welby, of whom the sole record is, that he "lived there forty years without being seen of any." In fact, it was a region of holes and corners, calculated to illustrate that great advantage of London life, which a friend of Boswell's described by saying, that a man could there be always " close to his burrow." The "burrow" which received the luckless wight, was indeed no pleasant refuge. Since poor Green, in the earliest generation of dramatists, bought his " groat'sworth of wit with a million of repentance," too many of his brethren had trodden the path which led to hopeless misery or death in a tavern brawl. The history of men who had to support themselves by their pens, is a record of almost universal gloom. The names of Spenser, of Butler, and of Otway, are enough to remind us that even warm contemporary recognition was not enough to raise an author above the fear of dying in want of necessaries. The two great dictators of literature, Ben Jonson in the earlier and Dryden in the later part of the century, only kept their heads above water by help of the laureate's pittance, though reckless imprudence, encouraged by the precarious life, was the cause of much of their sufferings. Patronage gave but a fitful resource, and the author could hope at most but an occasional crust, flung to him from better provided tables.

In the happy days of Queen Anne, it is true, there had been a gleam of prosperity. Many authors, Addison, Congreve, Swift, and others of less name, had won by their pens not only temporary profits but permanent

c

places. The class which came into power at the Revolution was willing for a time, to share some of the public patronage with men distinguished for intellectual eminence. Patronage was liberal when the funds came out of other men's pockets. But, as the system of party government developed, it soon became evident that this involved a waste of power. There were enough political partisans to absorb all the comfortable sinecures to be had ; and such money as was still spent upon literature, was given in return for services equally degrading to giver and receiver. Nor did the patronage of literature reach the poor inhabitants of Grub Street. Addison's poetical power might suggest or justify the gift of a place from his elegant friends ; but a man like De Foe, who really looked to his pen for great part of his daily subsistence, was below the region of such prizes, and was obliged in later years not only to write inferior books for money, but to sell himself and act as a spy upon his fellows. One great man, it is true, made an independence by literature. Pope received some £8000 for his translation of Homer, by the then popular mode of subscription—a kind of compromise between the systems of patronage and public support. But his success caused little pleasure in Grub Street. No love was lost between the poet and the dwellers in this dismal region. Pope was its deadliest enemy, and carried on an internecine warfare with its inmates, which has enriched our language with a great satire, but which wasted his powers upon low objects, and tempted him into disgraceful artifices. The life of the unfortunate victims, pilloried in the *Dunciad* and accused of the unpardonable sins of poverty and dependence, was too often one which might have extorted sympathy even from a thin-skinned poet and critic.

Illustrations of the manners and customs of that Grub

Street of which Johnson was to become an inmate are only
too abundant. The best writers of the day could tell of
hardships endured in that dismal region.   Richardson
went on the sound principle of keeping his shop that his
shop might keep him. But the other great novelists of
the century have painted from life the miseries of an
author's existence. Fielding, Smollett, and Goldsmith
have described the poor wretches with a vivid force which
gives sadness to the reflection that each of those great men
was drawing upon his own experience, and that they each
died in distress. The *Case of Authors by Profession*
to quote the title of a pamphlet by Ralph, was indeed a
wretched one, when the greatest of their number had an
incessant struggle to keep the wolf from the door. The
life of an author resembled the proverbial existence of the
flying-fish, chased by enemies in sea and in air; he only
escaped from the slavery of the bookseller's garret, to fly
from the bailiff or rot in the debtor's ward or the spunging-
house. Many strange half-pathetic and half-ludicrous anecdotes survive to recall the sorrows and the recklessness of
the luckless scribblers who, like one of Johnson's acquaintance, "lived in London and hung loose upon society."

There was Samuel Boyse, for example, whose poem on
the *Deity* is quoted with high praise by Fielding.   Once
Johnson had generously exerted himself for his comrade in
misery, and collected enough money by sixpences to get
the poet's clothes out of pawn. Two days afterwards,
Boyse had spent the money and was found in bed, covered
only with a blanket, through two holes in which he passed
his arms to write. Boyse, it appears, when still in this position would lay out his last half-guinea to buy truffles and
mushrooms for his last scrap of beef. Of another scribbler
Johnson said, " I honour Derrick for his strength of mind.

One night when Floyd (another poor author) was wander-
ing about the streets at night, he found Derrick fast asleep
upon a bulk.   Upon being suddenly awaked, Derrick
started up ; 'My dear Floyd, I am sorry to see you in this
destitute state; will you go home with me to my *lodgings?*' "
Authors in such circumstances might be forced into such
a wonderful contract as that which is reported to have
been drawn up by one Gardner with Rolt and Christopher
Smart.   They were to write a monthly miscellany, sold at
sixpence, and to have a third of the profits ; but they were
to write nothing else, and the contract was to last for
ninety-nine years.   Johnson himself summed up the trade
upon earth by the lines in which Virgil describes the
entrance to hell ; thus translated by Dryden :—

> Just in the gate and in the jaws of hell,
> Revengeful cares and sullen sorrows dwell.
> And pale diseases and repining age,
> Want, fear, and famine's unresisted rage :
> Here toils and Death and Death's half-brother, Sleep—
> Forms, terrible to view, their sentry keep.

" Now," said Johnson, " almost all these apply exactly
to an author; these are the concomitants of a printing-
house."

Judicious authors, indeed, were learning how to make
literature pay.   Some of them belonged to the class who
understood the great truth that the scissors are a very
superior implement to the pen considered as a tool of
literary trade.   Such, for example, was that respectable
Dr. John Campbell, whose parties Johnson ceased to frequent lest Scotchmen should say of any good bits of work,
" Ay, ay, he has learnt this of Cawmell."   Campbell, he said
quaintly, was a good man, a pious man.   " I am afraid he

has not been in the inside of a church for many years ;
but he never passes a church without pulling off his hat.
This shows he has good principles,"—of which in fact there
seems to be some less questionable evidence. Campbell supported himself by writings chiefly of the Encyclopedia or
Gazetteer kind ; and became, still in Johnson's phrase, "the
richest author that ever grazed the common of literature."
A more singular and less reputable character was that
impudent quack, Sir John Hill, who, with his insolent
attacks upon the Royal Society, pretentious botanical and
medical compilations, plays, novels, and magazine articles,
has long sunk into utter oblivion. It is said of him that
he pursued every branch of literary quackery with greater
contempt of character than any man of his time, and that
he made as much as £1500 in a year ;—three times as
much, it is added, as any one writer ever made in the
same period.

The political scribblers—the Arnalls, Gordons, Trench-
ards, Guthries, Ralphs, and Amhersts, whose names meet
us in the notes to the *Dunciad* and in contemporary
pamphlets and newspapers—form another variety of the
class. Their general character may be estimated from
Johnson's classification of the " Scribbler for a Party " with
the " Commissioner of Excise," as the " two lowest of all
human beings." " Ralph," says one of the notes to the
Dunciad, " ended in the common sink of all such writers,
a political newspaper." The prejudice against such employment has scarcely died out in our own day, and may
be still traced in the account of Pendennis and his friend
Warrington. People who do dirty work must be paid for
it ; and the Secret Committee which inquired into Walpole's administration reported that in ten years, from 1731
to 1741, a sum of £50,077 18s. had been paid to writers

and printers of newspapers. Arnall, now remembered chiefly by Pope's line,—

Spirit of Arnall, aid me whilst I lie!

had received, in four years, £10,997 6s. 8d. of this amount. The more successful writers might look to pensions or preferment. Francis, for example, the translator of Horace, and the father, in all probability, of the most formidable of the whole tribe of such literary gladiators, received, it is said, 900l. a year for his work, besides being appointed to a rectory and the chaplaincy of Chelsea.

It must, moreover, be observed that the price of literary work was rising during the century, and that, in the latter half, considerable sums were received by successful writers. Religious as well as dramatic literature had begun to be commercially valuable. Baxter, in the previous century, made from 60l. to 80l. a year by his pen. The copyright of Tillotson's *Sermons* was sold, it is said, upon his death for £2500. Considerable sums were made by the plan of publishing by subscription. It is said that 4600 people subscribed to the two posthumous volumes of Conybeare's *Sermons*. A few poets trod in Pope's steps. Young made more than £3000 for the Satires called the *Universal Passion*, published, I think, on the same plan ; and the Duke of Wharton is said, though the report is doubtful, to have given him £2000 for the same work. Gay made £1000 by his *Poems ;* £400 for the copyright of the *Beggar's Opera*, and three times as much for its second part, *Polly*. Among historians, Hume seems to have received £700 a volume ; Smollett made £2000 by his catchpenny rival publication ; Henry made £3300 by his history ; and Robertson, after the booksellers had made £6000 by his *History of Scotland*, sold his *Charles V.* for £4500.

Amongst the novelists, Feilding received £700 for *Tom Jones* and £1000 for *Amelia ;* Sterne, for the second edition of the first part of *Tristram Shandy* and for two additional volumes, received £650 ; besides which Lord Fauconberg gave him a living (most inappropriate acknowledgment, one would say!), and Warburton a purse of gold. Goldsmith received 60 guineas for the immortal *Vicar*, a fair price, according to Johnson, for a work by a then unknown author. By each of his plays he made about £500, and for the eight volumes of his *Natural History* he received 800 guineas. Towards the end of the century, Mrs. Radcliffe got £500 for the *Mysteries of Udolpho*, and £800 for her last work, the *Italian*. Perhaps the largest sum given for a single book was £6000 paid to Hawkesworth for his account of the South Sea Expeditions. Horne Tooke received from £4000 to £5000 for the *Diversions of Purley ;* and it is added by his biographer, though it seems to be incredible, that Hayley received no less than £11,000 for the *Life of Cowper*. This was, of course, in the present century, when we are already approaching the period of Scott and Byron.

Such sums prove that some few authors might achieve independence by a successful work ; and it is well to remember them in considering Johnson's life from the business point of view. Though he never grumbled at the booksellers, and on the contrary, was always ready to defend them as liberal men, he certainly failed, whether from carelessness or want of skill, to turn them to as much profit as many less celebrated rivals. Meanwhile, pecuniary success of this kind was beyond any reasonable hopes. A man who has to work like his own dependent Levett, and to make the " modest toil of every day" supply " the wants of every day," must discount his talents until he can secure leisure for some more sustained effort. Johnson, coming up from the country to seek for work, could have but a slender prospect of rising above the ordinary level of his Grub Street companions and rivals. One publisher to whom he applied suggested to him that it would be his wisest course to buy a porter's knot and carry trunks ; and, in the struggle which followed, Johnson must sometimes have been tempted to regret that the advice was not taken.

The details of the ordeal through which he was now to pass have naturally vanished. Johnson, long afterwards, burst into tears on recalling the trials of this period. But, at the time, no one was interested in noting the history of an obscure literary drudge, and it has not been described by the sufferer himself. What we know is derived from a few letters and incidental references of Johnson in later days. On first arriving in London he was almost destitute, and had to join with Garrick in raising a loan of five pounds, which, we are glad to say, was repaid. He dined for eightpence at an ordinary : a cut of meat for sixpence, bread for a penny, and a penny to the waiter, making out the charge. One of his acquaintance had told him that a man might live in London for thirty pounds a year. Ten pounds would pay for clothes ; a garret might be hired for eighteen-pence a week ; if any one asked for an address, it was easy to reply, " I am to be found at such a place." Threepence laid out at a coffee-house would enable him to pass some hours a day in good company ; dinner might be had for sixpence, a bread-and-milk breakfast for a penny, and supper was superfluous. On clean shirt day you might go abroad and pay visits. This leaves a surplus of nearly one pound from the thirty.

Johnson, however, had a wife to support; and to raise funds for even so ascetic a mode of existence required steady labour. Often, it seems, his purse was at the very lowest ebb. One of his letters to his employer is signed *impransus*; and whether or not the dinnerless condition was in this case accidental, or significant of absolute impecuniosity, the less pleasant interpretation is not improbable. He would walk the streets all night with his friend, Savage, when their combined funds could not pay for a lodging. One night, as he told Sir Joshua Reynolds in later years, they thus perambulated St. James's Square, warming themselves by declaiming against Walpole, and nobly resolved that they would stand by their country.

Patriotic enthusiasm, however, as no one knew better than Johnson, is a poor substitute for bed and supper. Johnson suffered acutely and made some attempts to escape from his misery. To the end of his life, he was grateful to those who had lent him a helping hand. "Harry Hervey," he said of one of them shortly before his death, "was a vicious man, but very kind to me. If you call a dog Hervey, I shall love him." Pope was impressed by the excellence of his first poem, *London*, and induced Lord Gower to write to a friend to beg Swift to obtain a degree for Johnson from the University of Dublin. The terms of this circuitous application, curious, as bringing into connexion three of the most eminent men of letters of the day, prove that the youngest of them was at the time (1739) in deep distress. The object of the degree was to qualify Johnson for a mastership of £60 a year, which would make him happy for life. He would rather, said Lord Gower, die upon the road to Dublin if an examination were necessary, "than be starved to death in translating for booksellers, which has been his only subsistence for some time past." The application failed, however, and the want of a degree was equally fatal to another application to be admitted to practise at Doctor's Commons.

Literature was thus perforce Johnson's sole support; and by literature was meant, for the most part, drudgery of the kind indicated by the phrase, " translating for booksellers." While still in Lichfield, Johnson had, as I have said, written to Cave, proposing to become a contributor to the *Gentleman's Magazine*. The letter was one of those which a modern editor receives by the dozen, and answers as perfunctorily as his conscience will allow. It seems, however, to have made some impression upon Cave, and possibly led to Johnson's employment by him on his first arrival in London. From 1738 he was employed both on the Magazine and in some jobs of translation.

Edward Cave, to whom we are thus introduced, was a man of some mark in the history of literature. Johnson always spoke of him with affection and afterwards wrote his life in complimentary terms. Cave, though a clumsy, phlegmatic person of little cultivation, seems to have been one of those men who, whilst destitute of real critical powers, have a certain instinct for recognizing the commercial value of literary wares. He had become by this time well-known as the publisher of a magazine which survives to this day. Journals containing summaries of passing events had already been started. Boyer's *Political State of Great Britain* began in 1711. *The Historical Register*, which added to a chronicle some literary notices, was started in 1716. *The Grub Street Journal* was another journal with fuller critical notices, which first appeared in 1730; and these two seem to have been superseded by the *Gentleman's Magazine*, started by Cave in the next year.

Johnson saw in it an opening for the employment of his
literary talents ; and regarded its contributors with that
awe so natural in youthful aspirants, and at once so comic
and pathetic to writers of a little experience. The names
of many of Cave's staff are preserved in a note to Hawkins.
One or two of them, such as Birch and Akenside, have
still a certain interest for students of literature ; but few
have heard of the great Moses Browne, who was regarded
as the great poetical light of the magazine. Johnson
looked up to him as a leader in his craft, and was
graciously taken by Cave to an alehouse in Clerkenwell,
where, wrapped in a horseman's coat, and " a great bushy
uncombed wig," he saw Mr. Browne sitting at the end of
a long table, in a cloud of tobacco-smoke, and felt the
satisfaction of a true hero-worshipper.

It is needless to describe in detail the literary task-work
done by Johnson at this period, the Latin poems which
he contributed in praise of Cave, and of Cave's friends, or
the Jacobite squibs by which he relieved his anti-minis-
terialist feelings. One incident of the period doubtless
refreshed the soul of many authors, who have shared
Campbell's gratitude to Napoleon for the sole redeeming
action of his life—the shooting of a bookseller. Johnson
was employed by Osborne, a rough specimen of the trade,
to make a catalogue of the Harleian Library. Osborne
offensively reproved him for negligence, and Johnson
knocked him down with a folio. The book with which
the feat was performed (*Biblia Græca Septuaginta, fol.*
1594, Frankfort) was in existence in a bookseller's shop at
Cambridge in 1812, and should surely have been placed
in some safe author's museum.

The most remarkable of Johnson's performances as a
hack writer deserves a brief notice. He was one of the

first of reporters. Cave published such reports of the
debates in Parliament as were then allowed by the
jealousy of the Legislature, under the title of *The Senate
of Lilliput.* Johnson was the author of the debates from
Nov. 1740 to February 1742. Persons were employed to
attend in the two Houses, who brought home notes of the
speeches, which were then put into shape by Johnson.
Long afterwards, at a dinner at Foote's, Francis (the father
of Junius) mentioned a speech of Pitt's as the best he
had ever read, and superior to anything in Demosthenes.
Hereupon Johnson replied, " I wrote that speech in a
garret in Exeter Street." When the company applauded
not only his eloquence but his impartiality, Johnson
replied, " That is not quite true ; I saved appearances
tolerably well, but I took care that the Whig dogs should
not have the best of it." The speeches passed for a time
as accurate ; though, in truth, it has been proved and it is
easy to observe, that they are, in fact, very vague
reflections of the original. The editors of Chesterfield's
Works published two of the speeches, and, to Johnson's
considerable amusement, declared that one of them resembled Demosthenes and the other Cicero. It is plain
enough to the modern reader that, if so, both of the
ancient orators must have written true Johnsonese ; and, in
fact, the style of the true author is often as plainly marked
in many of these compositions as in the *Rambler* or
Rasselas. For this deception, such as it was, Johnson
expressed penitence at the end of his life, though he said
that he had ceased to write when he found that they were
taken as genuine. He would not be " accessory to the
propagation of falsehood."

Another of Johnson's works which appeared in 1744
requires notice both for its intrinsic merit, and its auto-

biographical interest.   The most remarkable of his Grub-
Street companions was the Richard Savage already mentioned.   Johnson's life of him written soon after his death
is one of his most forcible performances, and the best extant
illustration of the life of the struggling authors of the
time.   Savage claimed to be the illegitimate son of the
Countess of Macclesfield, who was divorced from her husband in the year of his birth on account of her connexion
with his supposed father, Lord Rivers.   According to the
story, believed by Johnson, and published without her
contradiction in the mother's lifetime, she not only dis-
avowed her son, but cherished an unnatural hatred for
him.   She told his father that he was dead, in order that
he might not be benefited by the father's will ; she tried
to have him kidnapped and sent to the plantations ; and
she did her best to prevent him from receiving a pardon
when he had been sentenced to death for killing a man in a
tavern brawl.   However this may be, and there are reasons
for doubt, the story was generally believed, and caused
much sympathy for the supposed victim.   Savage was at
one time protected by the kindness of Steele, who published
his story, and sometimes employed him as a literary
assistant.   When Steele became disgusted with him, he
received generous help from the actor Wilks and from Mrs.
Oldfield, to whom he had been introduced by some dramatic efforts.   Then he was taken up by Lord Tyrconnel, but
abandoned by him after a violent quarrel ; he afterwards
called himself a volunteer laureate, and received a pension
of 50l. a year from Queen Caroline ; on her death he was
thrown into deep distress, and helped by a subscription
to which Pope was the chief contributor, on condition of
retiring to the country.   Ultimately he quarrelled with his
last protectors, and ended by dying in a debtor's prison.

Various poetical works, now utterly forgotten, obtained
for him scanty profit. This career sufficiently reveals the
character. Savage belonged to the very common type of
men, who seem to employ their whole talents to throw away
their chances in life, and to disgust every one who offers
them a helping hand. He was, however, a man of some
talent, though his poems are now hopelessly unreadable,
and seems to have had a singular attraction for Johnson.
The biography is curiously marked by Johnson's constant
effort to put the best face upon faults, which he has too
much love of truth to conceal. The explanation is, partly,
that Johnson conceived himself to be avenging a victim of
cruel oppression. " This mother," he says, after recording
her vindictiveness, " is still alive, and may perhaps even
yet, though her malice was often defeated, enjoy the
pleasure of reflecting that the life, which she often endeavoured to destroy, was at last shortened by her maternal
offices ; that though she could not transport her son to the
plantations, bury him in the shop of a mechanic, or hasten
the hand of the public executioner, she has yet had the
satisfaction of embittering all his hours, and forcing him
into exigencies that hurried on his death."

But it is also probable that Savage had a strong influence
upon Johnson's mind at a very impressible part of his
career. The young man, still ignorant of life and full of
reverent enthusiasm for the literary magnates of his time,
was impressed by the varied experience of his companion,
and, it may be, flattered by his intimacy. Savage, he says
admiringly, had enjoyed great opportunities of seeing the
most conspicuous men of the day in their private life. He
was shrewd and inquisitive enough to use his opportunities
well. " More circumstances to constitute a critic on human
life could not easily concur." The only phrase which survives

to justify this remark is Savage's statement about Walpole, that "the whole range of his mind was from obscenity to politics, and from politics to obscenity." We may, however, guess what was the special charm of the intercourse to Johnson. Savage was an expert in that science of human nature, learnt from experience not from books, upon which Johnson set so high a value, and of which he was destined to become the authorized expositor. There were, moreover, resemblances between the two men. They were both admired and sought out for their conversational powers. Savage, indeed, seems to have lived chiefly by the people who entertained him for talk, till he had disgusted them by his insolence and his utter disregard of time and propriety. He would, like Johnson, sit up talking beyond midnight, and next day decline to rise till dinner-time, though his favourite drink was not, like Johnson's, free from intoxicating properties. Both of them had a lofty pride, which Johnson heartily commends in Savage, though he has difficulty in palliating some of its manifestations. One of the stories reminds us of an anecdote already related of Johnson himself. Some clothes had been left for Savage at a coffeehouse by a person who, out of delicacy, concealed his name. Savage, however, resented some want of ceremony, and refused to enter the house again till the clothes had been removed.

What was honourable pride in Johnson was, indeed, simple arrogance in Savage. He asked favours, his biographer says, without submission, and resented refusal as an insult. He had too much pride to acknowledge, but not too much to receive, obligations; enough to quarrel with his charitable benefactors, but not enough to make him rise to independence of their charity. His pension would have sufficed to keep him, only that as soon as he received it he retired from the sight of all his acquaintance, and came back before long as penniless as before. This conduct, observes his biographer, was "very particular." It was hardly so singular as objectionable; and we are not surprised to be told that he was rather a "friend of goodness" than himself a good man. In short, we may say of him as Beauclerk said of a friend of Boswell's that, if he had excellent principles, he did not wear them out in practice.

There is something quaint about this picture of a thorough-paced scamp, admiringly painted by a virtuous man; forced, in spite of himself, to make it a likeness, and striving in vain to make it attractive. But it is also pathetic when we remember that Johnson shared some part at least of his hero's miseries. "On a bulk, in a cellar, or in a glass-house, among thieves and beggars, was to be found the author of *The Wanderer*, the man of exalted sentiments, extensive views, and curious observations; the man whose remarks on life might have assisted the statesman, whose ideas of virtue might have enlightened the moralist, whose eloquence might have influenced senators, and whose delicacy might have polished courts." Very shocking, no doubt, and yet hardly surprising under the circumstances! To us it is more interesting to remember that the author of the *Rambler* was not only a sympathizer, but a fellow-sufferer with the author of the *Wanderer*, and shared the queer "lodgings" of his friend, as Floyd shared the lodgings of Derrick. Johnson happily came unscathed through the ordeal which was too much for poor Savage, and could boast with perfect truth in later life that "no man, who ever lived by literature, had lived more independently than I have done." It was in so strange a school, and under such questionable teaching that Johnson formed his conception of the world and of the con-

duct befitting its inmates. · One characteristic conclusion
is indicated in the opening passage of the life. It has
always been observed, he says, that men eminent by nature
or fortune are not generally happy: "whether it be that
apparent superiority incites great designs, and great designs
are naturally liable to fatal miscarriages ; or that the general
lot of mankind is misery, and the misfortunes of those,
whose eminence drew upon them an universal attention,
have been more carefully recorded because they were more
generally observed, and have in reality been only more
conspicuous than those of others, not more frequent or
more severe."

The last explanation was that which really commended
itself to Johnson. Nobody had better reason to know
that obscurity might conceal a misery as bitter as any that
fell to the lot of the most eminent. The gloom due to his
constitutional temperament was intensified by the sense that
he and his wife were dependent upon the goodwill of a narrow and ignorant tradesman for the scantiest maintenance.
How was he to reach some solid standing-ground above the
hopeless mire of Grub Street? As a journeyman author
he could make both ends meet, but only on condition of
incessant labour. Illness and misfortune would mean
constant dependence upon charity or bondage to creditors.
To get ahead of the world it was necessary to distinguish
himself in some way from the herd of needy competitors.
He had come up from Lichfield with a play in his pocket,
but the play did not seem at present to have much chance
of emerging. Meanwhile he published a poem which did
something to give him a general reputation.

London—an imitation of the Third Satire of Juvenal—
was published in May, 1738. The plan was doubtless
suggested by Pope's imitations of Horace, which had

D

recently appeared. Though necessarily following the lines
of Juvenal's poem, and conforming to the conventional
fashion of the time, both in sentiment and versification,
the poem has a biographical significance. It is indeed
odd to find Johnson, who afterwards thought of London
as a lover of his mistress, and who despised nothing more
heartily than the cant of Rousseau and the sentimentalists,
adopting in this poem the ordinary denunciations of the
corruption of towns, and singing the praises of an innocent
country life. Doubtless, the young writer was like other
young men, taking up a strain still imitative and artificial.
He has a quiet smile at Savage in the life, because in his
retreat to Wales, that enthusiast declared that he " could
not debar himself from the happiness which was to be
found in the calm of a cottage, or lose the opportunity
of listening without intermission to the melody of the
nightingale, which he believed was to be heard from every
bramble, and which he did not fail to mention as a very
important part of the happiness of a country life." In
London, this insincere cockney adopts Savage's view.
Thales, who is generally supposed to represent Savage (and
this coincidence seems to confirm the opinion), is to retire
" from the dungeons of the Strand," and to end a healthy
life in pruning walks and twining bowers in his garden.

> There every bush with nature's music rings,
> There every breeze bears health upon its wings.

Johnson had not yet learnt the value of perfect sincerity
even in poetry. But it must also be admitted that London,
as seen by the poor drudge from a Grub Street garret, probably presented a prospect gloomy enough to make even
Johnson long at times for rural solitude. The poem reflects,
too, the ordinary talk of the heterogeneous band of patriots,

Jacobites, and disappointed Whigs, who were beginning to gather enough strength to threaten Walpole's long tenure of power. Many references to contemporary politics illustrate Johnson's sympathy with the inhabitants of the contemporary Cave of Adullam.

This poem, as already stated, attracted Pope's notice, who made a curious note on a scrap of paper sent with it to a friend. Johnson is described as " a man afflicted with an infirmity of the convulsive kind, that attacks him sometimes so as to make him a sad spectacle." This seems to have been the chief information obtained by Pope about the anonymous author, of whom he had said, on first reading the poem, this man will soon be *déterré*. *London* made a certain noise ; it reached a second edition in a week, and attracted various patrons, among others, General Oglethorpe, celebrated by Pope, and through a long life the warm friend of Johnson. One line, however, in the poem printed in capital letters, gives the moral which was doubtless most deeply felt by the author, and which did not lose its meaning in the years to come. This mournful truth, he says,—

Is everywhere confess'd,
Slow rises worth by poverty depress'd.

Ten years later (in January 1749) appeared the *Vanity of Human Wishes*, an imitation of the Tenth Satire of Juvenal. The difference in tone shows how deeply this and similar truths had been impressed upon its author in the interval. Though still an imitation, it is as significant as the most original work could be of Johnson's settled views of life. It was written at a white heat, as indeed Johnson wrote all his best work. Its strong Stoical morality, its profound and melancholy illustrations of the old and ever new sen-

timent, *Vanitas Vanitatum*, make it perhaps the most
impressive poem of the kind in the language. The lines
on the scholar's fate show that the iron had entered his
soul in the interval. Should the scholar succeed beyond
expectation in his labours and escape melancholy and
disease, yet, he says,—

> Yet hope not life from grief and danger free,
> Nor think the doom of man reversed on thee ;
> Deign on the passing world to turn thine eyes
> And pause awhile from letters, to be wise ;
> There mark what ills the scholar's life assail,
> Toil, envy, want, the patron and the jail ;
> See nations, slowly wise and meanly just,
> To buried merit raise the tardy bust.
> If dreams yet flatter, once again attend.
> Hear Lydiat's life and Galileo's end.

For the " patron," Johnson had originally written the
" garret." The change was made after an experience of
patronage to be presently described in connexion with
the *Dictionary*.

For *London* Johnson received ten guineas, and for the
Vanity of Human Wishes fifteen. Though indirectly
valuable, as increasing his reputation, such work was not
very profitable. The most promising career in a pecuniary
sense was still to be found on the stage. Novelists were
not yet the rivals of dramatists, and many authors had
made enough by a successful play to float them through a
year or two. Johnson had probably been determined by
his knowledge of this fact to write the tragedy of *Irene*.
No other excuse at least can be given for the composition
of one of the heaviest and most unreadable of dramatic
performances, interesting now, if interesting at all, solely
as a curious example of the result of bestowing great
powers upon a totally uncongenial task. Young men,

however, may be pardoned for such blunders if they are
not repeated, and Johnson, though he seems to have
retained a fondness for his unlucky performance, never
indulged in playwriting after leaving Lichfield. The best
thing connected with the play was Johnson's retort to his
friend Walmsley, the Lichfield registrar. " How," asked
Walmsley, " can you contrive to plunge your heroine into
deeper calamity ? " " Sir," said Johnson, " I can put her
into the spiritual court." Even Boswell can only say for
Irene that it is " entitled to the praise of superior excellence," and admits its entire absence of dramatic power.
Garrick, who had become manager of Drury Lane, produced his friend's work in 1749. The play was carried
through nine nights by Garrick's friendly zeal, so that the
author had his three nights' profits. For this he received
£195 17s. and for the copy he had £100. People probably attended, as they attend modern representations of
legitimate drama, rather from a sense of duty, than in the
hope of pleasure. The heroine originally had to speak
two lines with a bowstring round her neck. The situation
produced cries of murder, and she had to go off the stage
alive. The objectionable passage was removed, but *Irene*
was on the whole a failure, and has never, I imagine,
made another appearance. When asked how he felt upon
his ill-success, he replied " like the monument," and indeed
he made it a principle throughout life to accept the decision of the public like a sensible man without murmurs.

Meanwhile, Johnson was already embarked upon an
undertaking of a very different kind. In 1747 he had
put forth a plan for an English Dictionary, addressed
at the suggestion of Dodsley, to Lord Chesterfield, then
Secretary of State, and the great contemporary Mæcenas.
Johnson had apparently been maturing the scheme for

some time. "I know," he says in the "plan," that "the
work in which I engaged is generally considered as
drudgery for the blind, as the proper toil of artless
industry, a book that requires neither the light of learning
nor the activity of genius, but may be successfully performed without any higher quality than that of bearing
burdens with dull patience, and beating the track of the
alphabet with sluggish resolution." He adds in a sub-
sarcastic tone, that although princes and statesmen had
once thought it honourable to patronize dictionaries, he had
considered such benevolent acts to be "prodigies, recorded
rather to raise wonder than expectation," and he was accordingly pleased and surprised to find that Chesterfield
took an interest in his undertaking. He proceeds to lay
down the general principles upon which he intends to
frame his work, in order to invite timely suggestions and
repress unreasonable expectations. At this time, humble
as his aspirations might be, he took a view of the possi-
bilities open to him which had to be lowered before the
publication of the dictionary. He shared the illusion
that a language might be "fixed" by making a catalogue
of its words. In the preface which appeared with the
completed work, he explains very sensibly the vanity of
any such expectation. Whilst all human affairs are
changing, it is, as he says, absurd to imagine that the
language which repeats all human thoughts and feelings
can remain unaltered.

A dictionary, as Johnson conceived it, was in fact work
for a "harmless drudge," the definition of a lexicographer
given in the book itself. Etymology in a scientific sense
was as yet non-existent, and Johnson was not in this respect ahead of his contemporaries. To collect all the words
in the language, to define their meanings as accurately as

might be, to give the obvious or whimsical guesses at Etymology suggested by previous writers, and to append a good collection of illustrative passages was the sum of his ambition. Any systematic tracing of the historical processes by which a particular language had been developed was unknown, and of course the result could not be anticipated. The work, indeed, required a keen logical faculty of definition, and wide reading of the English literature of the two preceding centuries ; but it could of course give no play either for the higher literary faculties or faculties of scientific investigation. A dictionary in Johnson's sense was the highest kind of work to which a literary journeyman could be set, but it was still work for a journeyman, not for an artist. He was not adding to literature, but providing a useful implement for future men of letters.

Johnson had thus got on hand the biggest job that could be well undertaken by a good workman in his humble craft. He was to receive fifteen hundred and seventy-five pounds for the whole, and he expected to finish it in three years. The money, it is to be observed, was to satisfy not only Johnson but several copyists employed in the mechanical part of the work. It was advanced by instalments, and came to an end before the conclusion of the book. Indeed, it appeared when accounts were settled, that he had received a hundred pounds more than was due. He could, however, pay his way for the time, and would gain a reputation enough to ensure work in future. The period of extreme poverty had probably ended when Johnson got permanent employment on the *Gentleman's Magazine*. He was not elevated above the need of drudgery and economy, but he might at least be free from the dread of neglect. He could

command his market—such as it was. The necessity of
steady labour was probably useful in repelling his fits of
melancholy. His name was beginning to be known, and
men of reputation were seeking his acquaintance. In the
winter of 1749 he formed a club, which met weekly at a
"famous beef-steak house" in Ivy Lane. Among its
members were Hawkins, afterwards his biographer, and
two friends, Bathurst a physician, and Hawkesworth an
author, for the first of whom he entertained an unusually
strong affection. The Club, like its more famous successor,
gave Johnson an opportunity of displaying and improving
his great conversational powers. He was already dreaded
for his prowess in argument, his dictatorial manners and
vivid flashes of wit and humour, the more effective from
the habitual gloom and apparent heaviness of the dis-
courser.

The talk of this society probably suggested topics for
the *Rambler*, which appeared at this time, and caused
Johnson's fame to spread further beyond the literary circles
of London. The wit and humour have, indeed, left few
traces upon its ponderous pages, for the *Rambler* marks
the culminating period of Johnson's worst qualities of
style. The pompous and involved language seems indeed to
be a fit clothing for the melancholy reflections which are
its chief staple, and in spite of its unmistakable power it is
as heavy reading as the heavy class of lay-sermonizing to
which it belongs. Such literature, however, is often
strangely popular in England, and the *Rambler*, though
its circulation was limited, gave to Johnson his position
as a great practical moralist. He took his literary title,
one may say, from the *Rambler*, as the more familiar title
was derived from the *Dictionary*.

The *Rambler* was published twice a week from March

20th, 1750, to March 17th, 1752. In five numbers alone
he received assistance from friends, and one of these,
written by Richardson, is said to have been the only
number which had a large sale. The circulation rarely
exceeded 500, though ten English editions were published
in the author's lifetime, besides Scotch and Irish editions.
The payment, however, namely, two guineas a number,
must have been welcome to Johnson, and the friendship
of many distinguished men of the time was a still more
valuable reward. A quaint story illustrates the hero-
worship of which Johnson now became the object. Dr.
Burney, afterwards an intimate friend, had introduced
himself to Johnson by letter in consequence of the *Rambler*,
and the plan of the *Dictionary*. The admiration was
shared by a friend of Burney's, a Mr. Bewley, known—in
Norfolk at least—as the " philosopher of Massingham."
When Burney at last gained the honour of a personal
interview, he wished to procure some " relic " of Johnson
for his friend. He cut off some bristles from a hearth-
broom in the doctor's chambers, and sent them in a letter
to his fellow-enthusiast. Long afterwards Johnson was
pleased to hear of this simple-minded homage, and not
only sent a copy of the *Lives of the Poets* to the rural philosopher, but deigned to grant him a personal interview.

Dearer than any such praise was the approval of Johnson's wife. She told him that, well as she had thought of
him before, she had not considered him equal to such a
performance. The voice that so charmed him was soon to
be silenced for ever. Mrs. Johnson died (March 17th,
1752) three days after the appearance of the last *Rambler*.
The man who has passed through such a trial knows well
that, whatever may be in store for him in the dark future,
fate can have no heavier blow in reserve. Though John-

son once acknowledged to Boswell, when in a placid humour, that happier days had come to him in his old age than in his early life, he would probably have added that though fame and friendship and freedom from the harrowing cares of poverty might cause his life to be more equably happy, yet their rewards could represent but a faint and mocking reflection of the best moments of a happy marriage. His strong mind and tender nature reeled under the blow. Here is one pathetic little note written to the friend, Dr. Taylor, who had come to him in his distress. That which first announced the calamity, and which, said Taylor, " expressed grief in the strongest manner he had ever read," is lost.

" Dear Sir,—Let me have your company and instruction. Do not live away from me. My distress is great.

" Pray desire Mrs. Taylor to inform me what mourning I should buy for my mother and Miss Porter, and bring a note in writing with you.

" Remember me in your prayers, for vain is the help of man.

" I am, dear sir,

" SAM. JOHNSON."

We need not regret that a veil is drawn over the details of the bitter agony of his passage through the valley of the shadow of death. It is enough to put down the words which he wrote long afterwards when visibly approaching the close of all human emotions and interests : —

" This is the day on which, in 1752, dear Tetty died. I have now uttered a prayer of repentance and contrition ; perhaps Tetty knows that I prayed for her. Perhaps Tetty is now praying for me. God help me. Thou, God, art merciful, hear my prayers and enable me to trust in Thee.

"We were married almost seventeen years, and have now been parted thirty."

It seems half profane, even at this distance of time, to pry into grief so deep and so lasting. Johnson turned for relief to that which all sufferers know to be the only remedy for sorrow—hard labour. He set to work in his garret, an inconvenient room, " because," he said, " in that room only I never saw Mrs. Johnson." He helped his friend Hawkesworth in the *Adventurer*, a new periodical of the *Rambler* kind ; but his main work was the *Dictionary*, which came out at last in 1755. Its appearance was the occasion of an explosion of wrath which marks an epoch in our literature. Johnson, as we have seen, had dedicated the Plan to Lord Chesterfield ; and his language implies that they had been to some extent in personal communication. Chesterfield's fame is in curious antithesis to Johnson's. He was a man of great abilities, and seems to have deserved high credit for some parts of his statesmanship. As a Viceroy in Ireland in particular he showed qualities rare in his generation. To Johnson he was known as the nobleman who had a wide social influence as an acknowledged *arbiter elegantiarum*, and who reckoned among his claims some of that literary polish in which the earlier generation of nobles had certainly been superior to their successors. The art of life expounded in his *Letters* differs from Johnson's as much as the elegant diplomatist differs from the rough intellectual gladiator of Grub Street. Johnson spoke his mind of his rival without reserve. " I thought," he said, " that this man had been a Lord among wits ; but I find he is only a wit among Lords." And of the *Letters* he said more keenly that they taught the morals of a harlot and the manners of a dancing-master. Chesterfield's opinion of Johnson is indicated by the description

in his *Letters* of a "respectable Hottentot, who throws
his meat anywhere but down his throat." This absurd
person, said Chesterfield, "was not only uncouth in manners and warm in dispute, but behaved exactly in the
same way to superiors, equals, and inferiors; and therefore, by a necessary consequence, absurdly to two of the
three." *Hinc illæ lacrymæ !*

Johnson, in my opinion, was not far wrong in his judgment, though it would be a gross injustice to regard Chesterfield as nothing but a fribble. But men representing
two such antithetic types were not likely to admire each
other's good qualities. Whatever had been the intercourse
between them, Johnson was naturally annoyed when the
dignified noble published two articles in the *World*—a
periodical supported by such polite personages as himself
and Horace Walpole—in which the need of a dictionary
was set forth, and various courtly compliments described
Johnson's fitness for a dictatorship over the language.
Nothing could be more prettily turned ; but it meant, and
Johnson took it to mean, I should like to have the dictionary dedicated to me : such a compliment would add
a feather to my cap, and enable me to appear to the world
as a patron of literature as well as an authority upon manners. " After making great professions," as Johnson said,
" he had, for many years, taken no notice of me ; but when
my *Dictionary* was coming out, he fell a scribbling in the
World about it." Johnson therefore bestowed upon the
noble earl a piece of his mind in a letter which was not
published till it came out in Boswell's biography.

" My Lord,—I have been lately informed by the proprietor of the *World* that two papers, in which my *Dictionary* is recommended to the public, were written by
your lordship. To be so distinguished is an honour

which, being very little accustomed to favours from the great, I know not well how to receive, or in what terms to acknowledge.

" When, upon some slight encouragement, I first visited your Lordship, I was overpowered, like the rest of mankind, by the enchantment of your address ; and could not forbear to wish that I might boast myself, *le vainqueur du vainqueur de la terre*—that I might obtain that regard for which I saw the world contending; but I found my attendance so little encouraged that neither pride nor modesty would suffer me to continue it. When I had once addressed your Lordship in public, I had exhausted all the arts of pleasing which a retired and uncourtly scholar can possess. I had done all that I could ; and no man is well pleased to have his all neglected, be it ever so little.

" Seven years, my lord, have now passed, since I waited in your outward rooms and was repulsed from your door ; during which time I have been pushing on my work through difficulties of which it is useless to complain, and have brought it at last to the verge of publication without one act of assistance, one word of encouragement, and one smile of favour. Such treatment I did not expect, for I never had a patron before.

" The shepherd in *Virgil* grew at last acquainted with Love, and found him a native of the rocks.

" Is not a patron, my Lord, one who looks with unconcern on a man struggling for life in the water, and when he has reached the ground encumbers him with help ? The notice which you have been pleased to take of my labours, had it been early, had been kind ; but it has been delayed till I am indifferent, and cannot enjoy it ; till I am solitary, and cannot impart it ; till I am known, and

do not want it.   I hope it is no very cynical asperity not
to confess obligations where no benefit has been received,
or to be unwilling that the public should consider me as
owing that to a patron which Providence has enabled me
to do for myself.

" Having carried on my work thus far with so little
obligation to any favourer of learning, I shall not be disappointed though I should conclude it, should less be
possible, with less ; for I have been long wakened from
that dream of hope in which I once boasted myself with
so much exultation, my Lord,

" Your Lordship's most humble, most obedient servant,

" SAM. JOHNSON."

The letter is one of those knock-down blows to which
no answer is possible, and upon which comment is superfluous.   It was, as Mr. Carlyle calls it, " the far-famed
blast of doom proclaiming into the ear of Lord Chesterfield and through him, of the listening world, that patronage should be no more."

That is all that can be said ; yet perhaps it should be
added that Johnson remarked that he had once received
£10 from Chesterfield, though he thought the assistance
too inconsiderable to be mentioned in such a letter.   Hawkins also states that Chesterfield sent overtures to Johnson
through two friends, one of whom, long Sir Thomas Ro-
binson, stated that, if he were rich enough (a judicious
clause) he would himself settle £500 a year upon Johnson.
Johnson replied that if the first peer of the realm made
such an offer, he would show him the way downstairs.
Hawkins is startled at this insolence, and at Johnson's
uniform assertion that an offer of money was an insult.   We
cannot tell what was the history of the £10 ; but Johnson,
in spite of Hawkins's righteous indignation, was in fact too

proud to be a beggar, and owed to his pride his escape from the fate of Savage.

The appearance of the *Dictionary* placed Johnson in the position described soon afterwards by Smollett. He was henceforth "the great Cham of Literature"—a monarch sitting in the chair previously occupied by his namesake, Ben, by Dryden, and by Pope ; but which has since that time been vacant. The world of literature has become too large for such authority. Complaints were not seldom uttered at the time. Goldsmith has urged that Boswell wished to make a monarchy of what ought to be a republic. Goldsmith, who would have been the last man to find serious fault with the dictator, thought the dictatorship objectionable. Some time indeed was still to elapse before we can say that Johnson was firmly seated on the throne ; but the *Dictionary* and the *Rambler* had given him a position not altogether easy to appreciate, now that the *Dictionary* has been superseded and the *Rambler* gone out of fashion. His name was the highest at this time (1755) in the ranks of pure literature. The fame of Warburton possibly bulked larger for the moment, and one of his flatterers was comparing him to the Colossus which bestrides the petty world of contemporaries. But Warburton had subsided into episcopal repose, and literature had been for him a stepping-stone rather than an ultimate aim. Hume had written works of far more enduring influence than Johnson ; but they were little read though generally abused, and scarcely belong to the purely literary history. The first volume of his *History of England* had appeared (1754), but had not succeeded. The second was just coming out. Richardson was still giving laws to his little seraglio of adoring women; Fielding had died (1754), worn out by labour and dissipation ; Smollett was active in the literary

trade, but not in such a way as to increase his own dignity
or that of his employment; Gray was slowly writing a few
lines of exquisite verse in his retirement at Cambridge;
two young Irish adventurers, Burke and Goldsmith, were
just coming to London to try their fortune; Adam Smith
made his first experiment as an author by reviewing the
Dictionary in the *Edinburgh Review;* Robertson had not
yet appeared as a historian; Gibbon was at Lausanne
repenting of his old brief lapse into Catholicism as an act
of undergraduate's folly; and Cowper, after three years of
" giggling and making giggle" with Thurlow in an attorney's office, was now entered at the Temple and amusing
himself at times with literature in company with such
small men of letters as Colman, Bonnell Thornton, and
Lloyd.   It was a slack tide of literature; the generation
of Pope had passed away and left no successors, and no
writer of the time could be put in competition with the
giant now known as " Dictionary Johnson."

When the last sheet of the *Dictionary* had been carried
to the publisher, Millar, Johnson asked the messenger,
" What did he say? "   " Sir," said the messenger, " he
said, ' Thank God I have done with him.' "   " I am glad,"
replied Johnson, " that he thanks God for anything."
Thankfulness for relief from seven years' toil seems to have
been Johnson's predominant feeling: and he was not
anxious for a time to take any new labours upon his shoulders.   Some years passed which have left few traces either
upon his personal or his literary history.   He contributed a
good many reviews in 1756-7 to the *Literary Magazine,*
one of which, a review of Soame Jenyns, is amongst his
best performances.   To a weekly paper he contributed for
two years, from April, 1758, to April, 1760, a set of essays
called the *Idler,* on the old *Rambler* plan.   He did some

small literary cobbler's work, receiving a guinea for a
prospectus to a newspaper and ten pounds for correcting a
volume of poetry. He had advertised in 1756 a new
edition of Shakspeare which was to appear by Christmas,
1757 : but he dawdled over it so unconscionably that it
did not appear for nine years ; and then only in consequence of taunts from Churchill, who accused him with
too much plausibility of cheating his subscribers.

> He for subscribers baits his hook;
> And takes your cash : but where's the book ?
> No matter where ; wise fear, you know
> Forbids the robbing of a foe ;
> But what to serve our private ends
> Forbids the cheating of our friends ?

In truth, his constitutional indolence seems to have
gained advantages over him, when the stimulus of a heavy
task was removed. In his meditations, there are many
complaints of his "sluggishness" and resolutions of
amendment. "A kind of strange oblivion has spread
over me," he says in April, 1764, "so that I know not
what has become of the last years, and perceive that
incidents and intelligence pass over me without leaving
any impression."

It seems, however, that he was still frequently in
difficulties. Letters are preserved showing that in the
beginning of 1756, Richardson became surety for him for
a debt, and lent him six guineas to release him from
arrest. An event which happened three years later
illustrates his position and character. In January, 1759,
his mother died at the age of ninety. Johnson was
unable to come to Lichfield, and some deeply pathetic
letters to her and her stepdaughter, who lived with her,
record his emotions. Here is the last sad farewell upon
the snapping of the most sacred of human ties.

E

"Dear Honoured Mother," he says in a letter enclosed to Lucy Porter, the step-daughter, "neither your condition nor your character make it fit for me to say much. You have been the best mother, and I believe the best woman in the world. I thank you for your indulgence to me, and beg forgiveness of all that I have done ill, and of all that I have omitted to do well. God grant you His Holy Spirit, and receive you to everlasting happiness for Jesus Christ's sake. Amen. Lord Jesus receive your spirit. I am, dear, dear mother.

"Your dutiful son,
" Samuel Johnson."

Johnson managed to raise twelve guineas, six of them borrowed from his printer, to send to his dying mother. In order to gain money for her funeral expenses and some small debts, he wrote the story of *Rasselas*. It was composed in the evenings of a single week, and sent to press as it was written. He received £100 for this, perhaps the most successful of his minor writings, and £25 for a second edition. It was widely translated and universally admired. One of the strangest of literary coincidences is the contemporary appearance of this work and Voltaire's *Candide;* to which, indeed, it bears in some respects so strong a resemblance that, but for Johnson's apparent contradiction, we would suppose that he had at least heard some description of its design. The two stories, though widely differing in tone and style, are among the most powerful expressions of the melancholy produced in strong intellects by the sadness and sorrows of the world. The literary excellence of *Candide* has secured for it a wider and more enduring popularity than has fallen to the lot of Johnson's far heavier production. But

Rasselas is a book of singular force, and bears the most
characteristic impression of Johnson's peculiar temperament.

A great change was approaching in Johnson's circumstances. When George III. came to the throne, it struck
some of his advisers that it would be well, as Boswell puts
it, to open " a new and brighter prospect to men of literary
merit." This commendable design was carried out by
offering to Johnson a pension of three hundred a year.
Considering that such men as Horace Walpole and his
like were enjoying sinecures of more than twice as many
thousands for being their father's sons, the bounty does
not strike one as excessively liberal. It seems to have
been really intended as some set-off against other pensions
bestowed upon various hangers-on of the Scotch prime
minister, Bute. Johnson was coupled with the contemptible scribbler, Shebbeare, who had lately been in the
pillory for a Jacobite libel (a " he-bear " and a " she-bear,"
said the facetious newspapers), and when a few months
afterwards a pension of £200 a year was given to the old
actor, Sheridan, Johnson growled out that it was time for
him to resign his own. Somebody kindly repeated the
remark to Sheridan, who would never afterwards speak to
Johnson.

The pension, though very welcome to Johnson, who
seems to have been in real distress at the time, suggested
some difficulty. Johnson had unluckily spoken of a pension in his *Dictionary* as "generally understood to mean
pay given to a State hireling for treason to his country."
He was assured, however, that he did not come within
the definition; and that the reward was given for what
he had done, not for anything that he was expected to do.
After some hesitation, Johnson consented to accept the

payment thus offered without the direct suggestion of any obligation, though it was probably calculated that he would in case of need, be the more ready, as actually happened, to use his pen in defence of authority. He had not compromised his independence and might fairly laugh at angry comments. " I wish," he said afterwards, " that my pension were twice as large, that they might make twice as much noise." " I cannot now curse the House of Hanover," was his phrase on another occasion : " but I think that the pleasure of cursing the House of Hanover and drinking King James's health, are amply overbalanced by three hundred pounds a year." In truth, his Jacobitism was by this time, whatever it had once been, nothing more than a humorous crotchet, giving opportunity for the expression of Tory prejudice.

"I hope you will now purge and live cleanly like a gentleman," was Beauclerk's comment upon hearing of his friend's accession of fortune, and as Johnson is now emerging from Grub Street, it is desirable to consider what manner of man was to be presented to the wider circles that were opening to receive him.

CHAPTER III

JOHNSON AND HIS FRIENDS.

IT is not till some time after Johnson had come into the
enjoyment of his pension, that we first see him through
the eyes of competent observers. The Johnson of our
knowledge, the most familiar figure to all students of
English literary history had already long passed the prime
of life, and done the greatest part of his literary work.
His character, in the common phrase, had been "formed"
years before ; as, indeed, people's characters are chiefly
formed in the cradle ; and, not only his character, but the
habits which are learnt in the great schoolroom of the
world were fixed beyond any possibility of change. The
strange eccentricities which had now become a second
nature, amazed the society in which he was for over
twenty years a prominent figure. Unsympathetic observers, those especially to whom the Chesterfield type
represented the ideal of humanity, were simply disgusted
or repelled. The man, they thought, might be in his
place at a Grub Street pot-house ; but had no business in
a lady's drawing-room. If he had been modest and
retiring, they might have put up with his defects ; but
Johnson was not a person whose qualities, good or bad,
were of a kind to be ignored. Naturally enough, the
fashionable world cared little for the rugged old giant.

"The great," said Johnson, "had tried him and given him up ; they had seen enough of him ; " and his reason was pretty much to the purpose. "Great lords and great ladies don't love to have their mouths stopped," especially not, one may add, by an unwashed fist.

It is easy to blame them now. Everybody can see that a saint in beggar's rags is intrinsically better than a sinner in gold lace. But the principle is one of those which serves us for judging the dead, much more than for regulating our own conduct. Those, at any rate, may throw the first stone at the Horace Walpoles and Chesterfields, who are quite certain that they would ask a modern Johnson to their houses. The trial would be severe. Poor Mrs. Boswell complained grievously of her husband's idolatry. "I have seen many a bear led by a man," she said ; "but I never before saw a man led by a bear." The truth is, as Boswell explains, that the sage's uncouth habits, such as turning the candles' heads downwards to make them burn more brightly, and letting the wax drop upon the carpet, "could not but be disagreeable to a lady."

He had other habits still more annoying to people of delicate perceptions. A hearty despiser of all affectations, he despised especially the affectation of indifference to the pleasures of the table. "For my part," he said, "I mind my belly very studiously and very carefully, for I look upon it that he who does not mind his belly will hardly mind anything else." Avowing this principle he would innocently give himself the airs of a scientific epicure. "I, madam," he said to the terror of a lady with whom he was about to sup, "who live at a variety of good tables, am a much better judge of cookery than any person who has a very tolerable cook, but lives much at home, for his palate is gradually adapted to the taste of his cook, whereas, madam, in trying by a wider range, I can more exquisitely judge." But his pretensions to exquisite taste are by no means borne out by independent witnesses. "He laughs," said Tom Davies, "like a rhinoceros," and he seems to have eaten like a wolf— savagely, silently, and with undiscriminating fury. He was not a pleasant object during this performance. He was totally absorbed in the business of the moment, a strong perspiration came out, and the veins of his forehead swelled. He liked coarse satisfying dishes—boiled pork and veal-pie stuffed with plums and sugar ; and in regard to wine, he seems to have accepted the doctrines of the critic of a certain fluid professing to be port, who asked, " What more can you want ? It is black, and it is thick, and it makes you drunk." Claret, as Johnson put it, " is the liquor for boys, and port for men ; but he who aspires to be a hero must drink brandy." He could, however, refrain, though he could not be moderate, and for all the latter part of his life, from 1766, he was a total abstainer. Nor, it should be added, does he ever appear to have sought for more than exhilaration from wine. His earliest intimate friend, Hector, said that he had never but once seen him drunk.

His appetite for more innocent kinds of food was equally excessive. He would eat seven or eight peaches before breakfast, and declared that he had only once in his life had as much wall-fruit as he wished. His con- sumption of tea was prodigious, beyond all precedent. Hawkins quotes Bishop Burnet as having drunk sixteen large cups every morning, a feat which would entitle him to be reckoned as a rival. " A hardened and shameless tea- drinker," Johnson called himself, who " with tea amuses the evenings, with tea solaces the midnights, and with tea

welcomes the mornings." One of his teapots, preserved by
a relic-hunter, contained two quarts, and he professed to
have consumed five and twenty cups at a sitting. Poor
Mrs. Thrale complains that he often kept her up making
tea for him till four in the morning. His reluctance to
go to bed was due to the fact that his nights were periods
of intense misery; but the vast potations of tea can
scarcely have tended to improve them.

The huge frame was clad in the raggedest of garments,
until his acquaintance with the Thrales led to a partial
reform. His wigs were generally burnt in front, from
his shortsighted knack of reading with his head close to
the candle; and at the Thrales, the butler stood ready to
effect a change of wigs as he passed into the dining-room.
Once or twice we have accounts of his bursting into unusual splendour. He appeared at the first representation
of *Irene* in a scarlet waistcoat laced with gold; and on one
of his first interviews with Goldsmith he took the trouble
to array himself decently, because Goldsmith was reported
to have justified slovenly habits by the precedent of the
leader of his craft. Goldsmith, judging by certain famous
suits, seems to have profited by the hint more than his
preceptor. As a rule, Johnson's appearance, before he
became a pensioner, was worthy of the proverbial manner
of Grub Street. Beauclerk used to describe how he had
once taken a French lady of distinction to see Johnson in
his chambers. On descending the staircase they heard a
noise like thunder. Johnson was pursuing them, struck
by a sudden sense of the demands upon his gallantry.
He brushed in between Beauclerk and the lady, and seizing
her hand conducted her to her coach. A crowd of people
collected to stare at the sage, dressed in rusty brown, with
a pair of old shoes for slippers, a shrivelled wig on the top

of his head, and with shirtsleeves and the knees of his breeches hanging loose. In those days, clergymen and physicians were only just abandoning the use of their official costume in the streets, and Johnson's slovenly habits were even more marked than they would be at present. "I have no passion for clean linen," he once remarked, and it is to be feared that he must sometimes have offended more senses than one.

In spite of his uncouth habits of dress and manners, Johnson claimed and, in a sense, with justice, to be a polite man. "I look upon myself," he said once to Boswell, "as a very polite man." He could show the stately courtesy of a sound Tory, who cordially accepts the principle of social distinction, but has far too strong a sense of self-respect to fancy that compliance with the ordinary conventions can possibly lower his own position. Rank of the spiritual kind was especially venerable to him. "I should as soon have thought of contradicting a bishop," was a phrase which marked the highest conceivable degree of deference to a man whom he respected. Nobody, again, could pay more effective compliments, when he pleased; and the many female friends who have written of him agree, that he could be singularly attractive to women. Women are, perhaps, more inclined than men to forgive external roughness in consideration of the great charm of deep tenderness in a thoroughly masculine nature. A characteristic phrase was his remark to Miss Monckton. She had declared, in opposition to one of Johnson's prejudices, that Sterne's writings were pathetic: "I am sure," she said, "they have affected me." "Why," said Johnson, smiling and rolling himself about, "that is because, dearest, you are a dunce!" When she mentioned this to him some time afterwards he replied: "Madam, if I had

thought so, I certainly should not have said it." The truth
could not be more neatly put.

Boswell notes, with some surprise, that when Johnson
dined with Lord Monboddo he insisted upon rising when
the ladies left the table, and took occasion to observe that
politeness was " fictitious benevolence," and equally useful
in common intercourse. Boswell's surprise seems to indicate that Scotchmen in those days were even greater bears
than Johnson. He always insisted, as Miss Reynolds tells
us, upon showing ladies to their carriages through Bolt
Court, though his dress was such that her readers would,
she thinks, be astonished that any man in his senses
should have shown himself in it abroad or even at home.
Another odd indication of Johnson's regard for good manners, so far as his lights would take him, was the extreme
disgust with which he often referred to a certain footman
in Paris, who used his fingers in place of sugar-tongs. So
far as Johnson could recognize bad manners he was polite
enough, though unluckily the limitation is one of considerable importance.

Johnson's claims to politeness were sometimes, it is true,
put in a rather startling form. " Every man of any education," he once said to the amazement of his hearers,
" would rather be called a rascal than accused of deficiency
in the graces." Gibbon, who was present, slily inquired
of a lady whether among all her acquaintance she could
not find *one* exception. According to Mrs. Thrale, he went
even further. Dr. Barnard, he said, was the only man
who had ever done justice to his good breeding ; "and you
may observe," he added, " that I am well-bred to a degree
of needless scrupulosity." He proceeded, according to
Mrs. Thrale, but the report a little taxes our faith, to claim
the virtues not only of respecting ceremony, but of never

contradicting or interrupting his hearers.   It is rather odd
that Dr. Barnard had once a sharp altercation with Johnson, and avenged himself by a sarcastic copy of verses in
which, after professing to learn perfections from different
friends, he says,—

> Johnson shall teach me how to place,
> In varied light, each borrow'd grace;
>   From him I'll learn to write;
> Copy his clear familiar style,
> And by the roughness of his file,
>   Grow, like himself, polite.

Johnson, on this as on many occasions, repented of the
blow as soon as it was struck, and sat down by Barnard,
"literally smoothing down his arms and knees," and be-
seeching pardon.   Barnard accepted his apologies, but
went home and wrote his little copy of verses.

Johnson's shortcomings in civility were no doubt due,
in part, to the narrowness of his faculties of perception.
He did not know, for he could not see, that his uncouth
gestures and slovenly dress were offensive; and he was
not so well able to observe others as to shake off the manners contracted in Grub Street.   It is hard to study a
manual of etiquette late in life, and for a man of Johnson's
imperfect faculties it was probably impossible.   Errors of
this kind were always pardonable, and are now simply
ludicrous.   But Johnson often shocked his companions by
more indefensible conduct.   He was irascible, overbearing,
and, when angry, vehement beyond all propriety.   He was
a "tremendous companion," said Garrick's brother; and
men of gentle nature, like Charles Fox, often shrank from
his company, and perhaps exaggerated his brutality.

Johnson, who had long regarded conversation as the
chief amusement, came in later years to regard it as almost

the chief employment of life ; and he had studied the art
with the zeal of a man pursuing a favourite hobby. He
had always, as he told Sir Joshua Reynolds, made it a
principle to talk on all occasions as well as he could. He
had thus obtained a mastery over his weapons which made
him one of the most accomplished of conversational gladiators. He had one advantage which has pretty well
disappeared from modern society, and the disappearance of
which has been destructive to excellence of talk. A good
talker, even more than a good orator, implies a good audience. Modern society is too vast and too restless to give
a conversationalist a fair chance. For the formation of
real proficiency in the art, friends should meet often, sit
long, and be thoroughly at ease. A modern audience
generally breaks up before it is well warmed through, and
includes enough strangers to break the magic circle of social
electricity. The clubs in which Johnson delighted were
excellently adapted to foster his peculiar talent. There a
man could " fold his legs and have his talk out "—a pleasure hardly to be enjoyed now. And there a set of friends
meeting regularly, and meeting to talk, learnt to sharpen
each other's skill in all dialectic manœuvres. Conversation
may be pleasantest, as Johnson admitted, when two friends
meet quietly to exchange their minds without any thought
of display. But conversation considered as a game, as a
bout of intellectual sword-play, has also charms which
Johnson intensely appreciated. His talk was not of the
encyclopædia variety, like that of some more modern cele-
brities ; but it was full of apposite illustrations and unrivalled in keen argument, rapid flashes of wit and humour,
scornful retort and dexterous sophistry. Sometimes he
would fell his adversary at a blow ; his sword, as Boswell
said, would be through your body in an instant without

preliminary flourishes ; and in the excitement of talking
for victory, he would use any device that came to hand.
" There is no arguing with Johnson," said Goldsmith,
quoting a phrase from Cibber, " for if his pistol misses
fire, he knocks you down with the butt-end of it."

Johnson's view of conversation is indicated by his
remark about Burke. " That fellow," he said at a time of
illness, " calls forth all my powers. Were I to see Burke
now, it would kill me." " It is when you come close to a
man in conversation," he said on another occasion, " that
you discover what his real abilities are. To make a speech
in an assembly is a knack. Now I honour Thurlow, sir ;
Thurlow is a fine fellow, he fairly puts his mind to yours."

Johnson's retorts were fair play under the conditions of
the game, as it is fair play to kick an opponent's shins at
football. But of course a man who had, as it were, become the acknowledged champion of the ring, and who
had an irascible and thoroughly dogmatic temper, was
tempted to become unduly imperious. In the company of
which Savage was a distinguished member, one may guess
that the conversational fervour sometimes degenerated into
horse-play. Want of arguments would be supplied by per-
sonality, and the champion would avenge himself by brutality on an opponent who happened for once to be getting
the best of him. Johnson, as he grew older and got into
more polished society, became milder in his manners ; but
he had enough of the old spirit left in him to break forth
at times with ungovernable fury, and astonish the well-
regulated minds of respectable ladies and gentlemen.

Anecdotes illustrative of this ferocity abound, and his
best friends—except, perhaps, Reynolds and Burke—had
all to suffer in turn. On one occasion, when he had made
a rude speech even to Reynolds, Boswell states, though with

some hesitation, his belief that Johnson actually blushed.
The records of his contests in this kind fill a large space
in Boswell's pages. That they did not lead to worse consequences shows his absence of rancour. He was always
ready and anxious for a reconciliation, though he would
not press for one if his first overtures were rejected. There
was no venom in the wounds he inflicted, for there was no
ill-nature ; he was rough in the heat of the struggle, and in
such cases careless in distributing blows ; but he never enjoyed giving pain. None of his tiffs ripened into permanent
quarrels, and he seems scarcely to have lost a friend. He
is a pleasant contrast in this, as in much else, to Horace
Walpole, who succeeded, in the course of a long life, in
breaking with almost all his old friends. No man set a
higher value upon friendship than Johnson. " A man," he
said to Reynolds, " ought to keep his friendship in constant
repair ;" or he would find himself left alone as he grew
older. " I look upon a day as lost," he said later in life,
" in which I do not make a new acquaintance." Making
new acquaintances did not involve dropping the old. The
list of his friends is a long one, and includes, as it were,
successive layers, superposed upon each other, from the
earliest period of his life.

This is so marked a feature in Johnson's character, that
it will be as well at this point to notice some of the friendships from which he derived the greatest part of his
happiness. Two of his schoolfellows, Hector and Taylor,
remained his intimates through life. Hector survived to give
information to Boswell, and Taylor, then a prebendary of
Westminster, read the funeral service over his old friend
in the Abbey. He showed, said some of the bystanders,
too little feeling. The relation between the two men was
not one of special tenderness ; indeed they were so little

congenial that Boswell rather gratuitously suspected his
venerable teacher of having an eye to Taylor's will. It
seems fairer to regard the acquaintance as an illustration
of that curious adhesiveness which made Johnson cling to
less attractive persons. At any rate, he did not show the
complacence of the proper will-hunter. Taylor was rector
of Bosworth and squire of Ashbourne. He was a fine
specimen of the squire-parson ; a justice of the peace, a
warm politician, and what was worse, a warm Whig. He
raised gigantic bulls, bragged of selling cows for 120
guineas and more, and kept a noble butler in purple clothes
and a large white wig. Johnson respected Taylor as a
sensible man, but was ready to have a round with him on
occasion. He snorted contempt when Taylor talked of
breaking some small vessels if he took an emetic. " Bah,"
said the doctor, who regarded a valetudinarian as a " scoundrel," " if you have so many things that will break, you
had better break your neck at once, and there's an end
on't." Nay, if he did not condemn Taylor's cows, he
criticized his bulldog with cruel acuteness. " No, sir, he
is not well shaped ; for there is not the quick transition
from the thickness of the fore-part to the *tenuity*—the
thin part—behind, which a bulldog ought to have." On the
more serious topic of politics his Jacobite fulminations
roused Taylor " to a pitch of bellowing." Johnson roared
out that if the people of England were fairly polled (this
was in 1777) the present king would be sent away to-night,
and his adherents hanged to-morrow. Johnson, however,
rendered Taylor the substantial service of writing sermons
for him, two volumes of which were published after they
were both dead ; and Taylor must have been a bold man,
if it be true, as has been said, that he refused to preach a
sermon written by Johnson upon Mrs. Johnson's death, on

the ground that it spoke too favourably of the character
of the deceased.

Johnson paid frequent visits to Lichfield, to keep up his
old friends. One of them was Lucy Porter, his wife's
daughter, with whom, according to Miss Seward, he had
been in love before he married her mother. He was at least
tenderly attached to her through life. And, for the most
part, the good people of Lichfield seem to have been proud
of their fellow-townsman, and gave him a substantial proof
of their sympathy by continuing to him, on favourable terms,
the lease of a house originally granted to his father. There
was, indeed, one remarkable exception in Miss Seward,
who belonged to a genus specially contemptible to the
old doctor. She was one of the fine ladies who dabbled
in poetry, and aimed at being the centre of a small literary
circle at Lichfield. Her letters are amongst the most
amusing illustrations of the petty affectations and squabbles
characteristic of such a provincial clique. She evidently
hated Johnson at the bottom of her small soul; and, indeed, though Johnson once paid her a preposterous compliment—a weakness of which this stern moralist was apt
to be guilty in the company of ladies—he no doubt trod
pretty roughly upon some of her pet vanities.

By far the most celebrated of Johnson's Lichfield friends
was David Garrick, in regard to whom his relations were
somewhat peculiar. Reynolds said that Johnson considered Garrick to be his own property, and would never
allow him to be praised or blamed by any one else without
contradiction. Reynolds composed a pair of imaginary
dialogues to illustrate the proposition, in one of which
Johnson attacks Garrick in answer to Reynolds, and in the
other defends him in answer to Gibbon. The dialogues
seem to be very good reproductions of the Johnsonian

manner, though perhaps the courteous Reynolds was a little too much impressed by its roughness ; and they probably include many genuine remarks of Johnson's. It is remarkable that the praise is far more pointed and elaborate than the blame, which turns chiefly upon the general inferiority of an actor's position. And, in fact, this seems to have corresponded to Johnson's opinion about Garrick as gathered from Boswell.

The two men had at bottom a considerable regard for each other, founded upon old association, mutual services, and reciprocal respect for talents of very different orders. But they were so widely separated by circumstances, as well as by a radical opposition of temperament, that any close intimacy could hardly be expected. The bear and the monkey are not likely to be intimate friends. Garrick's rapid elevation in fame and fortune seems to have produced a certain degree of envy in his old schoolmaster. A grave moral philosopher has, of course, no right to look askance at the rewards which fashion lavishes upon men of lighter and less lasting merit, and which he professes to despise. Johnson, however, was troubled with a rather excessive allowance of human nature. Moreover he had the good old-fashioned contempt for players, characteristic both of the Tory and the inartistic mind. He asserted roundly that he looked upon players as no better than dancing-dogs. " But, sir, you will allow that some players are better than others ? " " Yes, sir, as some dogs dance better than others." So when Goldsmith accused Garrick of grossly flattering the queen, Johnson exclaimed, " And as to meanness—how is it mean in a player, a showman, a fellow who exhibits himself for a shilling, to flatter his queen ? " At another time Boswell suggested that we might respect a great player. " What ! sir," exclaimed Johnson, " a

F

fellow who claps a hump upon his back and a lump on his leg and cries, '*I am Richard III.*' ? Nay, sir, a ballad-singer is a higher man, for he does two things : he repeats and he sings ; there is both recitation and music in his performance—the player only recites."

Such sentiments were not very likely to remain unknown to Garrick nor to put him at ease with Johnson, whom, indeed, he always suspected of laughing at him. They had a little tiff on account of Johnson's Edition of Shakspeare. From some misunderstanding, Johnson did not make use of Garrick's collection of old plays. Johnson, it seems, thought that Garrick should have courted him more, and perhaps sent the plays to his house; whereas Garrick, knowing that Johnson treated books with a roughness ill-suited to their constitution, thought that he had done quite enough by asking Johnson to come to his library. The revenge—if it was revenge—taken by Johnson was to say nothing of Garrick in his Preface, and to glance obliquely at his non-communication of his rarities. He seems to have thought that it would be a lowering of Shakspeare to admit that his fame owed anything to Garrick's exertions.

Boswell innocently communicated to Garrick a criticism of Johnson's upon one of his poems—

I'd smile with the simple and feed with the poor.

"Let me smile with the wise, and feed with the rich," was Johnson's tolerably harmless remark. Garrick, however, did not like it, and when Boswell tried to console him by saying that Johnson gored everybody in turn, and added, "*fœnum habet in cornu.*" "Ay," said Garrick vehemently, "he has a whole mow of it."

The most unpleasant incident was when Garrick proposed
rather too freely to be a member of the Club. Johnson
said that the first duke in England had no right to use
such language, and said, according to Mrs. Thrale, " If
Garrick does apply, I'll blackball him. Surely we ought
to be able to sit in a society like ours—

> ' Unelbowed by a gamester, pimp, or player ! ' "

Nearly ten years afterwards, however, Johnson favoured
his election, and when he died, declared that the Club
should have a year's widowhood. No successor to Garrick
was elected during that time.

Johnson sometimes ventured to criticise Garrick's acting,
but here Garrick could take his full revenge. The pur-
blind Johnson was not, we may imagine, much of a critic
in such matters. Garrick reports him to have said of an
actor at Lichfield, " There is a courtly vivacity about the
fellow ;" when, in fact, said Garrick, " he was the most
vulgar ruffian that ever went upon boards."

In spite of such collisions of opinion and mutual
criticism, Johnson seems to have spoken in the highest
terms of Garrick's good qualities, and they had many
pleasant meetings. Garrick takes a prominent part in two
or three of the best conversations in Boswell, and seems
to have put his interlocutors in specially good temper.
Johnson declared him to be " the first man in the world for
sprightly conversation." He said that Dryden had written
much better prologues than any of Garrick's, but that
Garrick had written more good prologues than Dryden. He
declared that it was wonderful how little Garrick had been
spoilt by all the flattery that he had received. No wonder
if he was a little vain : " a man who is perpetually flattered

in every mode that can be conceived : so many bellows have
blown the fuel, that one wonders he is not by this time become
a cinder !"   "If all this had happened to me," he said on
another occasion, " I should have had a couple of fellows
with long poles walking before me, to knock down everybody
that stood in the way.   Consider, if all this had happened
to Cibber and Quin, they'd have jumped over the moon.
Yet Garrick speaks to us," smiling.   He admitted at the
same time that Garrick had raised the profession of a
player.   He defended Garrick, too, against the common
charge of avarice.   Garrick, as he pointed out, had been
brought up in a family whose study it was to make four-
pence go as far as fourpence-halfpenny.   Johnson remembered in early days drinking tea with Garrick when Peg
Woffington made it, and made it, as Garrick grumbled, " as
red as blood."   But when Garrick became rich he became
liberal.   He had, so Johnson declared, given away more
money than any man in England.

    After Garrick's death, Johnson took occasion to say, in
the *Lives of the Poets*, that the death "had eclipsed the
gaiety of nations and diminished the public stock of harmless pleasures."   Boswell ventured to criticise the observation rather spitefully.   " Why *nations ?* Did his gaiety
extend further than his own nation ? "   " Why, sir," replied
Johnson, " some exaggeration must be allowed.   Besides,
we may say *nations* if we allow the Scotch to be a nation,
and to have gaiety—which they have not."   On the whole,
in spite of various drawbacks, Johnson's reported observations upon Garrick will appear to be discriminative, and
yet, on the whole, strongly favourable to his character.
Yet we are not quite surprised that Mrs. Garrick did not
respond to a hint thrown out by Johnson, that he would
be glad to write the life of his friend.

At Oxford, Johnson acquired the friendship of Dr. Adams, afterwards Master of Pembroke and author of a once well-known reply to Hume's argument upon miracles. He was an amiable man, and was proud to do the honours of the university to his old friend, when, in later years, Johnson revisited the much-loved scenes of his neglected youth. The warmth of Johnson's regard for old days is oddly illustrated by an interview recorded by Boswell with one Edwards, a fellow-student whom he met again in 1778, not having previously seen him since 1729. They had lived in London for forty years without once meeting, a fact more surprising then than now. Boswell eagerly gathered up the little scraps of college anecdote which the meeting produced, but perhaps his best find was a phrase of Edwards himself. " You are a philosopher, Dr. Johnson," he said ; " I have tried, too, in my time to be a philosopher ; but, I don't know how, cheerfulness was always breaking in." The phrase, as Boswell truly says, records an exquisite trait of character.

Of the friends who gathered round Johnson during his period of struggle, many had vanished before he became well known. The best loved of all seems to have been Dr. Bathurst, a physician, who, failing to obtain practice, joined the expedition to Havannah, and fell a victim to the climate (1762). Upon him Johnson pronounced a panegyric which has contributed a proverbial phrase to the language. " Dear Bathurst," he said, " was a man to my very heart's content : he hated a fool and he hated a rogue, and he hated a Whig ; he was a *very good hater*." Johnson remembered Bathurst in his prayers for years after his loss, and received from him a peculiar legacy. Francis Barber had been the negro slave of Bathurst's father, who left him his liberty by will. Dr. Bathurst allowed him to enter

Johnson's service; and Johnson sent him to school at considerable expense, and afterwards retained him in his
service with little interruption till his own death. Once
Barber ran away to sea, and was discharged, oddly enough,
by the good offices of Wilkes, to whom Smollett applied
on Johnson's behalf. Barber became an important member
of Johnson's family, some of whom reproached him for his
liberality to the nigger. No one ever solved the great
problem as to what services were rendered by Barber to
his master, whose wig was " as impenetrable by a comb as
a quickset hedge," and whose clothes were never touched
by the brush.

Among the other friends of this period must be
reckoned his biographer, Hawkins, an attorney who was
afterwards Chairman of the Middlesex Justices, and
knighted on presenting an address to the King. Boswell
regarded poor Sir John Hawkins with all the animosity of
a rival author, and with some spice of wounded vanity.
He was grievously offended, so at least says Sir John's
daughter, on being described in the *Life of Johnson* as
" Mr. James Boswell " without a solitary epithet such as
celebrated or well-known. If that was really his feelings
he had his revenge; for no one book ever so suppressed
another as Boswell's Life suppressed Hawkins's. In truth,
Hawkins was a solemn prig, remarkable chiefly for the
unusual intensity of his conviction that all virtue consists
in respectability. He had a special aversion to " goodness
of heart," which he regarded as another name for a quality
properly called extravagance or vice. Johnson's tenacity of
old acquaintance introduced him into the Club, where he
made himself so disagreeable, especially, as it seems, by
rudeness to Burke, that he found it expedient to invent a
pretext for resignation. Johnson called him a " very un-

clubable man," and may perhaps have intended him in the quaint description : " I really believe him to be an honest man at the bottom ; though, to be sure, he is rather penurious, and he is somewhat mean ; and it must be owned he has some degree of brutality, and is not without a tendency to savageness that cannot well be defended."

In a list of Johnson's friends it is proper to mention Richardson and Hawkesworth. Richardson seems to have given him substantial help, and was repaid by favourable comparisons with Fielding, scarcely borne out by the verdict of posterity. " Fielding," said Johnson, " could tell the hour by looking at the clock ; whilst Richardson knew how the clock was made." " There is more knowledge of the heart," he said at another time, " in one letter of Richardson's than in all *Tom Jones*." Johnson's preference of the sentimentalist to the man whose humour and strong sense were so like his own, shows how much his criticism was biassed by his prejudices ; though, of course, Richardson's external decency was a recommendation to the moralist. Hawkesworth's intimacy with Johnson seems to have been chiefly in the period between the *Dictionary* and the pension. He was considered to be Johnson's best imitator ; and has vanished like other imitators. His fate, if the very doubtful story believed at the time be true, was a curious one for a friend of Johnson's. He had made some sceptical remarks as to the efficacy of prayer in his preface to the South Sea Voyages ; and was so bitterly attacked by a " Christian" in the papers, that he destroyed himself by a dose of opium.

Two younger friends, who became disciples of the sage soon after the appearance of the *Rambler*, are prominent figures in the later circle. One of these was Bennet Langton, a man of good family, fine scholarship, and very

amiable character. His exceedingly tall and slender figure
was compared by Best to the stork in Raphael's cartoon of
the Miraculous Draught of Fishes. Miss Hawkins describes
him sitting with one leg twisted round the other as though
to occupy the smallest possible space, and playing with his
gold snuff-box with a mild countenance and sweet smile.
The gentle, modest creature was loved by Johnson, who
could warm into unusual eloquence in singing his praises.
The doctor, however, was rather fond of discussing with
Boswell the faults of his friend. They seem to have chiefly
consisted in a certain languor or sluggishness of temperament which allowed his affairs to get into perplexity. Once,
when arguing the delicate question as to the propriety of
telling a friend of his wife's unfaithfulness, Boswell, after
his peculiar fashion, chose to enliven the abstract statement
by the purely imaginary hypothesis of Mr. and Mrs. Langton being in this position. Johnson said that it would
be useless to tell Langton, because he would be too sluggish
to get a divorce. Once Langton was the unconscious
cause of one of Johnson's oddest performances. Langton
had employed Chambers, a common friend of his and
Johnson's, to draw his will. Johnson, talking to Chambers and Boswell, was suddenly struck by the absurdity
of his friend's appearing in the character of testator. His
companions, however, were utterly unable to see in what
the joke consisted ; but Johnson laughed obstreperously
and irrepressibly : he laughed till he reached the Temple
Gate ; and when in Fleet Street went almost into convulsions of hilarity. Holding on by one of the posts in the
street, he sent forth such peals of laughter that they seemed
in the silence of the night to resound from Temple Bar to
Fleet Ditch.

Not long before his death, Johnson applied to Langton

for spiritual advice. " I desired him to tell me sincerely
in what he thought my life was faulty." Langton wrote
upon a sheet of paper certain texts recommending Christian
charity ; and explained, upon inquiry, that he was pointing
at Johnson's habit of contradiction. The old doctor began
by thanking him earnestly for his kindness ; but gradually
waxed savage and asked Langton, " in a loud and angry
tone, What is your drift, sir ? " He complained of the well-
meant advice to Boswell, with a sense that he had been
unjustly treated. It was a scene for a comedy, as Reynolds observed, to see a penitent get into a passion and
belabour his confessor.

Through Langton, Johnson became acquainted with the
friend whose manner was in the strongest contrast to his
own. Topham Beauclerk was a man of fashion. He was
commended to Johnson by a likeness to Charles II., from
whom he was descended, being the grandson of the first
Duke of St. Alban's. Beauclerk was a man of literary and
scientific tastes. He inherited some of the moral laxity
which Johnson chose to pardon in his ancestor. Some
years after his acquaintance with Boswell he married Lady
Diana Spencer, a lady who had been divorced upon his
account from her husband, Lord Bolingbroke. But he
took care not to obtrude his faults of life, whatever they
may have been, upon the old moralist, who entertained
for him a peculiar affection. He specially admired Beauclerk's skill in the use of a more polished, if less vigorous,
style of conversation than his own. He envied the ease
with which Beauclerk brought out his sly incisive retorts.
" No man," he said, " ever was so free when he was going
to say a good thing, from a look that expressed that it was
coming ; or, when he had said it, from a look that expressed that it had come." When Beauclerk was dying

(in 1780), Johnson said, with a faltering voice, that he
would walk to the extremity of the diameter of the earth
to save him. Two little anecdotes are expressive of his
tender feeling for this incongruous friend. Boswell had
asked him to sup at Beauclerk's. He started, but, on the
way, recollecting himself, said, "I cannot go ; but *I do
not love Beauclerk the less.*" Beauclerk had put upon a
portrait of Johnson the inscription,—

> Ingenium ingens
> Inculto latet hoc sub corpore.

Langton, who bought the portrait, had the inscription
removed. "It was kind in you to take it off," said
Johnson; and, after a short pause, "not unkind in him to
put it on."

Early in their acquaintance, the two young men, Beau
and Lanky, as Johnson called them, had sat up one night
at a tavern till three in the morning. The courageous
thought struck them that they would knock up the old
philosopher. He came to the door of his chambers, poker
in hand, with an old wig for a nightcap. On hearing their
errand, the sage exclaimed, "What! is it you, you dogs?
I'll have a frisk with you." And so Johnson with the
two youths, his juniors by about thirty years, proceeded
to make a night of it. They amazed the fruiterers in
Covent Garden ; they brewed a bowl of bishop in a tavern,
while Johnson quoted the poet's address to Sleep,—

> "Short, O short, be then thy reign,
> And give us to the world again!"

They took a boat to Billingsgate, and Johnson, with
Beauclerk, kept up their amusement for the following day,
when Langton deserted them to go to breakfast with some

young ladies, and Johnson scolded him for leaving his friends "to go and sit with a parcel of wretched *unidea'd* girls." "I shall have my old friend to bail out of the round-house," said Garrick when he heard of this queer alliance; and he told Johnson that he would be in the *Chronicle* for his frolic. "He *durst* not do such a thing. His wife would not let him," was the moralist's retort.

Some friends, known to fame by other titles than their connexion with Johnson, had by this time gathered round them. Among them was one, whose art he was unable to appreciate, but whose fine social qualities and dignified equability of temper made him a valued and respected companion. Reynolds had settled in London at the end of 1752. Johnson met him at the house of Miss Cotterell. Reynolds had specially admired Johnson's *Life of Savage*, and, on their first meeting, happened to make a remark which delighted Johnson. The ladies were regretting the loss of a friend to whom they were under obligations. "You have, however," said Reynolds, "the comfort of being relieved from a burden of gratitude." The saying is a little too much like Rochefoucauld, and too true to be pleasant; but it was one of those keen remarks which Johnson appreciated because they prick a bubble of commonplace moralizing without demanding too literal an acceptation. He went home to sup with Reynolds and became his intimate friend. On another occasion, Johnson was offended by two ladies of rank at the same house, and by way of taking down their pride, asked Reynolds in a loud voice, "How much do you think you and I could get in a week, if we both worked as hard as we could?" "His appearance," says Sir Joshua's sister, Miss Reynolds, "might suggest the poor author: as he was not likely in that place to be a blacksmith or a porter." Poor Miss

Reynolds, who tells this story, was another attraction to
Reynolds' house. She was a shy, retiring maiden lady,
who vexed her famous brother by following in his steps
without his talents, and was deeply hurt by his annoyance
at the unintentional mockery. Johnson was through life
a kind and judicious friend to her ; and had attracted
her on their first meeting by a significant indication of his
character. He said that when going home to his lodgings
at one or two in the morning, he often saw poor children
asleep on thresholds and stalls—the wretched "street
Arabs" of the day—and that he used to put pennies into
their hands that they might buy a breakfast.

Two friends, who deserve to be placed beside Reynolds,
came from Ireland to seek their fortunes in London.
Edmund Burke, incomparably the greatest writer upon
political philosophy in English literature, the master of a
style unrivalled for richness, flexibility, and vigour, was
radically opposed to Johnson on party questions, though
his language upon the French Revolution, after Johnson's
death, would have satisfied even the strongest prejudices
of his old friend. But he had qualities which commended
him even to the man who called him a "bottomless
Whig," and who generally spoke of Whigs as rascals, and
maintained that the first Whig was the devil. If his
intellect was wider, his heart was as warm as Johnson's,
and in conversation he merited the generous applause and
warm emulation of his friend. Johnson was never tired of
praising the extraordinary readiness and spontaneity of
Burke's conversation. " If a man," he said, " went under
a shed at the same time with Burke to avoid a shower,
he would say, ' This is an extraordinary man.' Or if
Burke went into a stable to see his horse dressed, the ostler
would say, ' We have had an extraordinary man here.' "

When Burke was first going into Parliament, Johnson said in answer to Hawkins, who wondered that such a man should get a seat, " We who know Mr. Burke, know that he will be one of the first men in the country." Speaking of certain other members of Parliament, more after the heart of Sir John Hawkins, he said that he grudged success to a man who made a figure by a knowledge of a few forms, though his mind was " as narrow as the neck of a vinegar cruet;" but that he did not grudge Burke's being the first man in the House of Commons, for he would be the first man everywhere. And Burke equally admitted Johnson's supremacy in conversation. " It is enough for me," he said to some one who regretted Johnson's monopoly of the talk on a particular occasion, " to have rung the bell for him."

The other Irish adventurer, whose career was more nearly moulded upon that of Johnson, came to London in 1756, and made Johnson's acquaintance some time afterwards (in or before 1761). Goldsmith, like Johnson, had tasted the bitterness of an usher's life, and escaped into the scarcely more tolerable regions of Grub Street. After some years of trial, he was becoming known to the booksellers as a serviceable hand, and had two works in his desk destined to lasting celebrity. His landlady (apparently 1764) one day arrested him for debt. Johnson, summoned to his assistance, sent him a guinea and speedily followed. The guinea had already been changed, and Goldsmith was consoling himself with a bottle of Madeira. Johnson corked the bottle, and a discussion of ways and means brought out the manuscript of the *Vicar of Wakefield*. Johnson looked into it, took it to a bookseller, got sixty pounds for it, and returned to Goldsmith, who paid his rent and administered a sound rating to his landlady.

The relation thus indicated is characteristic ; Johnson
was as a rough but helpful elder brother to poor Goldsmith, gave him advice, sympathy, and applause, and at
times criticised him pretty sharply, or brought down his
conversational bludgeon upon his sensitive friend. " He
has nothing of the bear but his skin," was Goldsmith's
comment upon his clumsy friend, and the two men appreciated each other at bottom. Some of their readers may
be inclined to resent Johnson's attitude of superiority.
The admirably pure and tender heart, and the exquisite
intellectual refinement implied in the *Vicar* and the
Traveller, force us to love Goldsmith in spite of superficial foibles, and when Johnson prunes or interpolates
lines in the *Traveller*, we feel as though a woodman's axe
was hacking at a most delicate piece of carving. The
evidence of contemporary observers, however, must force
impartial readers to admit that poor Goldsmith's foibles
were real, however amply compensated by rare and admirable qualities. Garrick's assertion, that he " wrote like
an angel but talked like poor Poll," expresses the unani-
mous opinion of all who had actually seen him. Un-
doubtedly some of the stories of his childlike vanity, his
frankly expressed envy, and his general capacity for blundering, owe something to Boswell's feeling that he was
a rival near the throne, and sometimes poor Goldsmith's
humorous self-assertion may have been taken too seriously
by blunt English wits. One may doubt, for example,
whether he was really jealous of a puppet tossing a pike,
and unconscious of his absurdity in saying " Pshaw ! I
could do it better myself !" Boswell, however, was too
good an observer to misrepresent at random, and he has,
in fact, explained very well the true meaning of his
remarks. Goldsmith was an excitable Irishman of genius,

who tumbled out whatever came uppermost, and revealed the feelings of the moment with utter want of reserve. His self-controlled companions wondered, ridiculed, misinterpreted, and made fewer hits as well as fewer misses. His anxiety to "get in and share," made him, according to Johnson, an "unsocial" companion. Goldsmith, he said, had not temper enough for the game he played. He staked too much. A man might always get a fall from his inferior in the chances of talk, and Goldsmith felt his falls too keenly. He had certainly some trials of temper in Johnson's company. "Stay, stay," said a German, stopping him in the full flow of his eloquence, "Toctor Johnson is going to say something." An Eton Master called Graham, who was supping with the two doctors, and had got to the pitch of looking at one person, and talking to another, said, "Doctor, I shall be glad to see *you* at Eton." "I shall be glad to wait on you," said Goldsmith. "No," replied Graham, "'tis not you I mean, Doctor Minor; 'tis Doctor Major there." Poor Goldsmith said afterwards, "Graham is a fellow to make one commit suicide."

Boswell who attributes some of Goldsmith's sayings about Johnson to envy, said with probable truth that Goldsmith had not more envy than others, but only spoke of it more freely. Johnson argued that we must be angry with a man who had so much of an odious quality that he could not keep it to himself, but let it "boil over." The feeling, at any rate, was momentary and totally free from malice; and Goldsmith's criticisms upon Johnson and his idolators seem to have been fair enough. His objection to Boswell's substituting a monarchy for a republic has already been mentioned. At another time he checked Boswell's flow of panegyric by asking, " Is he like Burke,

who winds into a subject like a serpent?" To which
Boswell replied with charming irrelevance, "Johnson is
the Hercules who strangled serpents in his cradle." The
last of Goldsmith's hits was suggested by Johnson's
shaking his sides with laughter because Goldsmith admired
the skill with which the little fishes in the fable were made
to talk in character. "Why, Dr. Johnson, this is not so
easy as you seem to think," was the retort, "for if you were
to make little fishes talk, they would talk like whales."

In spite of sundry little sparrings, Johnson fully appreciated Goldsmith's genius. Possibly his authority hastened
the spread of public appreciation, as he seemed to claim,
whilst repudiating Boswell's too flattering theory that
it had materially raised Goldsmith's position. When
Reynolds quoted the authority of Fox in favour of the
Traveller, saying that his friends might suspect that they
had been too partial, Johnson replied very truly that the
Traveller was beyond the need of Fox's praise, and that
the partiality of Goldsmith's friends had always been
against him. They would hardly give him a hearing.
"Goldsmith," he added, "was a man who, whatever he
wrote, always did it better than any other man could
do." Johnson's settled opinion in fact was that embodied
in the famous epitaph with its "nihil tetigit quod non
ornavit," and, though dedications are perhaps the only
literary product more generally insincere than epitaphs, we
may believe that Goldsmith too meant what he said in the
dedication of *She Stoops to Conquer*. "It may do me
some honour to inform the public that I have lived many
years in intimacy with you. It may serve the interests
of mankind also to inform them that the greatest wit may
be found in a character, without impairing the most un-
affected piety."

Though Johnson was thus rich in friendship, two connexions have still to be noticed which had an exceptional
bearing upon his fame and happiness.   In January, 1765,
he made the acquaintance of the Thrales.   Mr. Thrale
was the proprietor of the brewery which afterwards
became that of Barclay and Perkins.   He was married in
1763 to a Miss Hester Lynch Salisbury, who has become
celebrated from her friendship with Johnson.[1]   She was
a woman of great vivacity and independence of character.
She had a sensitive and passionate, if not a very tender
nature, and enough literary culture to appreciate Johnson's
intellectual power, and on occasion to play a very respectable part in conversation.   She had far more Latin and
English scholarship than fell to the lot of most ladies of
her day, and wit enough to preserve her from degenerating
like some of the " blues," into that most offensive of
beings—a feminine prig.   Her marriage had been one of
convenience, and her husband's want of sympathy, and
jealousy of any interference in business matters, forced
her, she says, to take to literature as her sole resource.
" No wonder," she adds, " if I loved my books and
children."   It is, perhaps, more to be wondered at that
her children seem to have had a rather subordinate place
in her affections.   The marriage, however, though not of
the happiest, was perfectly decorous.   Mrs. Thrale discharged her domestic duties irreproachably, even when
she seems to have had some real cause of complaint.   To
the world she eclipsed her husband, a solid respectable
man, whose mind, according to Johnson, struck the hours
very regularly, though it did not mark the minutes.

[1] Mrs. Thrale was born in 1740 or 1741, probably the latter.
Thrale was born in 1724.

G

The Thrales were introduced to Johnson by their common friend, Arthur Murphy, an actor and dramatist, who afterwards became the editor 'of Johnson's works. One day, when calling upon Johnson, they found him in such a fit of despair that Thrale tried to stop his mouth by placing his hand before it. The pair then joined in begging Johnson to leave his solitary abode, and come to them at their country-house at Streatham. He complied, and for the next sixteen years a room was set apart for him, both at Streatham and in their house in Southwark. He passed a large part of his time with them, and derived from the intimacy most of the comfort of his later years. He treated Mrs. Thrale with a kind of paternal gallantry, her age at the time of their acquaintance being about twenty-four, and his fifty-five. He generally called her by the playful name of " my mistress," addressed little poems to her, gave her solid advice, and gradually came to confide to her his miseries and ailments with rather surprising frankness. She flattered and amused him, and soothed his sufferings and did something towards humanizing his rugged exterior. There was one little grievance between them which requires notice. Johnson's pet virtue in private life was a rigid regard for truth. He spoke, it was said of him, as if he was always on oath. He would not, for example, allow his servant to use the phrase " not at home," and even in the heat of conversation resisted the temptation to give point to an anecdote. The lively Mrs. Thrale rather fretted against the restraint, and Johnson admonished her in vain. He complained to Boswell that she was willing to have that said of her, which the best of mankind had died rather than have said of them. Boswell, the faithful imitator of his master in this respect, delighted in taking up the parable. " Now, madam, give

me leave to catch you in the fact," he said on one
occasion ; "it was not an old woman, but an old man whom
I mentioned, as having told me this," and he recounts his
check to the "lively lady" with intense complacency. As
may be imagined, Boswell and Mrs. Thrale did not love
each other, in spite of the well-meant efforts of the sage to
bring about a friendly feeling between his disciples.

It is time to close this list of friends with the inimitable
Boswell. James Boswell, born in 1740, was the eldest
son of a Whig laird and lord of sessions. He had acquired
some English friends at the Scotch universities, among
whom must be mentioned Mr. Temple, an English clergyman. Boswell's correspondence with Temple, discovered
years after his death by a singular chance, and published
in 1857, is, after the Life of Johnson, one of the most
curious exhibitions of character in the language. Boswell
was intended for the Scotch bar, and studied civil law at
Utrecht in the winter of 1762. It was in the following
summer that he made Johnson's acquaintance.

Perhaps the fundamental quality in Boswell's character
was his intense capacity for enjoyment. He was, as Mr.
Carlyle puts it, " gluttonously fond of whatever would
yield him a little solacement, were it only of a stomachic
character." His love of good living and good drink would
have made him a hearty admirer of his countryman,
Burns, had Burns been famous in Boswell's youth. Nobody could have joined with more thorough abandonment
in the chorus to the poet's liveliest songs in praise of love
and wine. He would have made an excellent fourth when
" Willie brewed a peck of maut, and Rab and Allan cam
to pree," and the drinking contest for the Whistle comme-
morated in another lyric would have excited his keenest
interest. He was always delighted when he could get

Johnson to discuss the ethics and statistics of drinking. "I am myself," he says, "a lover of wine, and therefore curious to hear whatever is remarkable concerning drinking." The remark is *à propos* to a story of Dr. Campbell drinking thirteen bottles of port at a sitting. Lest this should seem incredible, he quotes Johnson's dictum. "Sir, if a man drinks very slowly and lets one glass evaporate before he takes another, I know not how long he may drink." Boswell's faculty for making love was as great as his power of drinking. His letters to Temple record with amusing frankness the vicissitudes of some of his courtships and the versatility of his passions.

Boswell's tastes, however, were by no means limited to sensual or frivolous enjoyments. His appreciation of the bottle was combined with an equally hearty sensibility to more intellectual pleasures. He had not a spark of philosophic or poetic power, but within the ordinary range of such topics as can be discussed at a dinner-party, he had an abundant share of liveliness and intelligence. His palate was as keen for good talk as for good wine. He was an admirable recipient, if not an originator, of shrewd or humorous remarks upon life and manners. What in regard to sensual enjoyment was mere gluttony, appeared in higher matters as an insatiable curiosity. At times this faculty became intolerable to his neighbours. "I will not be baited with what and why," said poor Johnson, one day in desperation. "Why is a cow's tail long? Why is a fox's tail bushy?" "Sir," said Johnson on another occasion, when Boswell was cross-examining a third person about him in his presence. "You have but two subjects, yourself and me. I am sick of both." Boswell, however, was not to be repelled by such a retort as this, or even by ruder rebuffs. Once when discussing the means of getting a friend to leave London, Johnson said in revenge for a previous offence. " Nay, sir, we'll send you to him. If your presence doesn't drive a man out of his house, nothing will." Boswell was " horribly shocked," but he still stuck to his victim like a leech, and pried into the minutest details of his life and manners. He observed with conscientious accuracy that though Johnson abstained from milk one fast-day, he did not reject it when put in his cup. He notes the whistlings and puffings, the trick of saying " too-too-too " of his idol : and it was a proud day when he won a bet by venturing to ask Johnson what he did with certain scraped bits of orange-peel. His curiosity was not satisfied on this occasion ; but it would have made him the prince of interviewers in these days. Nothing delighted him so much as rubbing shoulders with any famous or notorious person. He scraped acquaintance with Voltaire, Wesley, Rousseau, and Paoli, as well as with Mrs. Rudd, a for-gotten heroine of the *Newgate Calendar*. He was as eager to talk to Hume the sceptic, or Wilkes the dema-gogue, as to the orthodox Tory, Johnson ; and, if repelled, it was from no deficiency in daring. In 1767, he took advantage of his travels in Corsica to introduce himself to Lord Chatham, then Prime Minister. The letter modestly ends by asking, " *Could your lordship find time to honour me now and then with a letter ?* I have been told how favourably your lordship has spoken of me. To correspond with a Paoli and with a Chatham is enough to keep a young man ever ardent in the pursuit of virtuous fame." No other young man of the day, we may be sure, would have dared to make such a proposal to the majestic orator.

His absurd vanity, and the greedy craving for notoriety

at any cost, would have made Boswell the most offensive
of mortals, had not his unfeigned good-humour disarmed
enmity. Nobody could help laughing, or be inclined to
take offence at his harmless absurdities. Burke said of
him that he had so much good-humour naturally, that it
was scarcely a virtue. His vanity, in fact, did not
generate affectation. Most vain men are vain of qualities
which they do not really possess, or possess in a lower
degree than they fancy. They are always acting a part,
and become touchy from a half-conscious sense of the
imposture. But Boswell seems to have had few such
illusions. He thoroughly and unfeignedly enjoyed his
own peculiarities, and thought his real self much too
charming an object to be in need of any disguise. No man,
therefore, was ever less embarrassed by any regard for his
own dignity. He was as ready to join in a laugh at himself as in a laugh at his neighbours. He reveals his own
absurdities to the world at large as frankly as Pepys confided them to a journal in cypher. He tells us how
drunk he got one night in Skye, and how he cured his
headache with brandy next morning ; and what an intolerable fool he made of himself at an evening party in
London after a dinner with the Duke of Montrose, and
how Johnson in vain did his best to keep him quiet. His
motive for the concession is partly the wish to illustrate
Johnson's indulgence, and, in the last case, to introduce a
copy of apologetic verses to the lady whose guest he had
been. He reveals other weaknesses with equal frankness.
One day, he says, "I owned to Johnson that I was
occasionally troubled with a fit of narrowness." " Why,
sir," said he, " so am I. *But I do not tell it.*" Boswell
enjoys the joke far too heartily to act upon the advice.

There is nothing, however, which Boswell seems to have

enjoyed more heartily than his own good impulses. He
looks upon his virtuous resolution with a sort of æsthetic
satisfaction, and with the glow of a virtuous man contem-
plating a promising penitent. Whilst suffering severely
from the consequences of imprudent conduct, he gets a
letter of virtuous advice from his friend Temple. He in-
stantly sees himself reformed for the rest of his days.
"My warm imagination," he says, "looks forward with
great complacency on the sobriety, the healthfulness, and
worth of my future life." "Every instance of our doing
those things which we ought not to have done, and leaving
undone those things which we ought to have done, is
attended," as he elsewhere sagely observes, "with more or
less of what is truly remorse ;" but he seems rather to have
enjoyed even the remorse. It is needless to say that the
complacency was its own reward, and that the resolution
vanished like other more eccentric impulses. Music, he
once told Johnson, affected him intensely, producing in
his mind "alternate sensations of pathetic dejection, so
that I was ready to shed tears, and of daring resolution
so that I was inclined to rush into the thickest of the
[purely hypothetical] battle." "Sir," replied Johnson,
"I should never hear it, if it made me such a fool."
Elsewhere he expresses a wish to "fly to the woods," or
retire into a desert, a disposition which Johnson checked
by one of his habitual gibes at the quantity of easily ac-
cessible desert in Scotland. Boswell is equally frank in
describing himself in situations more provocative of contempt than even drunkenness in a drawing-room. He
tells us how dreadfully frightened he was by a storm at sea
in the Hebrides, and how one of his companions, "with
a happy readiness," made him lay hold of a rope fastened
to the masthead, and told him to pull it when he was

ordered.   Boswell was thus kept quiet in mind and harmless in body.

This extreme simplicity of character makes poor Boswell loveable in his way.   If he sought notoriety, he did not so far mistake his powers as to set up for independent notoriety.[1] He was content to shine in reflected light: and the affectations with which he is charged seem to have been unconscious imitations of his great idol.   Miss Burney traced some likeness even in his dress.   In the later part of the *Life* we meet phrases in which Boswell is evidently aping the true Johnsonian style.   So, for example, when somebody distinguishes between "moral" and "physical necessity;" Boswell exclaims, "Alas, sir, they come both to the same thing.   You may be as hard bound by chains when covered by leather, as when the iron appears."   But he specially emulates the profound melancholy of his hero. He seems to have taken pride in his sufferings from hypochondria; though, in truth, his melancholy diverges from Johnson's by as great a difference as that which divides any two varieties in Jaques's classification.   Boswell's was the melancholy of a man who spends too much, drinks too much, falls in love too often, and is forced to live in the country in dependence upon a stern old parent, when he is longing for a jovial life in London taverns.   Still he was excusably vexed when Johnson refused to believe in the reality of his complaints, and showed scant sympathy to his noisy would-be fellow-sufferer.   Some of Boswell's freaks

---

[1] The story is often told how Boswell appeared at the Stratford Jubilee with "Corsica Boswell" in large letters on his hat.   The account given apparently by himself is sufficiently amusing, but the statement is not quite fair.   Boswell not unnaturally appeared at a masquerade in the dress of a Corsican chief, and the inscription on his hat seems to have been "Viva la Libertà."

were, in fact, very trying. Once he gave up writing letters
for a long time, to see whether Johnson would be induced
to write first. Johnson became anxious, though he half-
guessed the truth, and in reference to Boswell's confession
gave his disciple a piece of his mind. " Remember that
all tricks are either knavish or childish, and that it is as
foolish to make experiments upon the constancy of a friend
as upon the chastity of a wife."

In other ways Boswell was more successful in aping his
friend's peculiarities. When in company with Johnson, he
became delightfully pious. " My dear sir," he exclaimed
once with unrestrained fervour, " I would fain be a good
man, and I am very good now. I fear God and honour
the king ; I wish to do no ill and to be benevolent to all
mankind." Boswell hopes, " for the felicity of human
nature," that many experience this mood ; though Johnson
judiciously suggested that he should not trust too much to
impressions. In some matters Boswell showed a touch of
independence by outvying the Johnsonian prejudices. He
was a warm admirer of feudal principles, and especially
held to the propriety of entailing property upon heirs male.
Johnson had great difficulty in persuading him to yield to
his father's wishes, in a settlement of the estate which con-
travened this theory. But Boswell takes care to declare
that his opinion was not shaken. " Yet let me not be
thought," he adds, " harsh or unkind to daughters ; for my
notion is that they should be treated with great affection
and tenderness, and always participate of the prosperity
of the family." His estimate of female rights is indicated
in another phrase. When Mrs. Knowles, the Quaker,
expressed a hope that the sexes would be equal in another
world, Boswell replied, " That is too ambitious, madam.
We might as well desire to be equal with the angels."

Boswell, again, differed from Johnson—who, in spite of his love of authority, had a righteous hatred for all recognized tyranny—by advocating the slave-trade. To abolish that trade would, he says, be robbery of the masters and cruelty to the African savages. Nay, he declares, to abolish it would be

> To shut the gates of mercy on mankind!

Boswell was, according to Johnson, "the best travelling companion in the world." In fact, for such purposes, unfailing good-humour and readiness to make talk at all hazards are high recommendations. "If, sir, you were shut up in a castle and a new-born baby with you, what would you do?" is one of his questions to Johnson,—à *propos* of nothing. That is exquisitely ludicrous, no doubt; but a man capable of preferring such a remark to silence helps at any rate to keep the ball rolling. A more objectionable trick was his habit not only of asking preposterous or indiscreet questions, but of setting people by the ears out of sheer curiosity. The appearance of so queer a satellite excited astonishment among Johnson's friends. "Who is this Scotch cur at Johnson's heels?" asked some one. "He is not a cur," replied Goldsmith; "he is only a bur. Tom Davies flung him at Johnson in sport, and he has the faculty of sticking." The bur stuck till the end of Johnson's life. Boswell visited London whenever he could, and soon began taking careful notes of Johnson's talk. His appearance, when engaged in this task long afterwards, is described by Miss Burney. Boswell, she says, concentrated his whole attention upon his idol, not even answering questions from others. When Johnson spoke, his eyes goggled with eagerness; he leant his ear almost on the Doctor's shoulder; his mouth dropped open to catch every syllable; and he seemed to listen even to Johnson's breathings as though they had some mystical significance. He took every opportunity of edging himself close to Johnson's side even at meal-times, and was sometimes ordered imperiously back to his place like a faithful but over-obtrusive spaniel.

It is hardly surprising that Johnson should have been touched by the fidelity of this queer follower. Boswell, modestly enough, attributes Johnson's easy welcome to his interest in all manifestations of the human mind, and his pleasure in an undisguised display of its workings. The last pleasure was certainly to be obtained in Boswell's society. But in fact Boswell, though his qualities were too much those of the ordinary " good fellow," was not without virtues, and still less without remarkable talents. He was, to all appearance, a man of really generous sympathies, and capable of appreciating proofs of a warm heart and a vigorous understanding. Foolish, vain, and absurd in every way, he was yet a far kindlier and more genuine man than many who laughed at him. His singular gifts as an observer could only escape notice from a careless or inexperienced reader. Boswell has a little of the true Shaksperian secret. He lets his characters show themselves without obtruding unnecessary comment. He never misses the point of a story, though he does not ostentatiously call our attention to it. He gives just what is wanted to indicate character, or to explain the full meaning of a repartee. It is not till we compare his reports with those of less skilful hearers, that we can appreciate the skill with which the essence of a conversation is extracted, and the whole scene indicated by a few telling touches. We are tempted to fancy that we have heard the very thing, and rashly infer that Boswell was simply the mechanical trans-

mitter of the good things uttered.   Any one who will try to
put down the pith of a brilliant conversation within the
same space, may soon satisfy himself of the absurdity of such
an hypothesis, and will learn to appreciate Boswell's powers
not only of memory but artistic representation.   Such a
feat implies not only admirable quickness of appreciation,
but a rare literary faculty.   Boswell's accuracy is remarkable ; but it is the least part of his merit.

   The book which so faithfully reflects the peculiarities of
its hero and its author became the first specimen of a new
literary type.   Johnson himself was a master in one kind
of biography ; that which sets forth a condensed and
vigorous statement of the essentials of a man's life and
character.   Other biographers had given excellent memoirs
of men considered in relation to the chief historical currents
of the time.   But a full-length portrait of a man's domestic
life with enough picturesque detail to enable us to see
him through the eyes of private friendship did not exist
in the language.   Boswell's originality and merit may be
tested by comparing his book to the ponderous performance of Sir John Hawkins, or to the dreary dissertations,
falsely called lives, of which Dugald Stewart's *Life of
Robertson* may be taken for a type.   The writer is so
anxious to be dignified and philosophical that the despair-
ing reader seeks in vain for a single vivid touch, and
discovers even the main facts of the hero's life by some
indirect allusion.   Boswell's example has been more or
less followed by innumerable successors ; and we owe it
in some degree to his example that we have such delightful books as Lockhart's *Life of Scott* or Mr. Trevelyan's
Life of Macaulay.   Yet no later biographer has been quite
as fortunate in a subject ; and Boswell remains as not only
the first, but the best of his class.

One special merit implies something like genius. Macaulay
has given to the usual complaint which distorts the vision
of most biographers the name of *lues Boswelliana*. It is
true that Boswell's adoration of his hero is a typical example of the feeling. But that which distinguishes Boswell, and renders the phrase unjust, is that in him adoration
never hindered accuracy of portraiture. " I will not make
my tiger a cat to please anybody," was his answer to well-
meaning entreaties of Hannah More to soften his accounts
of Johnson's asperities. He saw instinctively that a man
who is worth anything loses far more than he gains by
such posthumous flattery. The whole picture is toned
down, and the lights are depressed as well as the shadows.
The truth is that it is unscientific to consider a man as a
bundle of separate good and bad qualities, of which one
half may be concealed without injury to the rest. Johnson's fits of bad temper, like Goldsmith's blundering, must
be unsparingly revealed by a biographer, because they are
in fact expressions of the whole character. It is necessary
to take them into account in order really to understand either
the merits or the shortcomings. When they are softened or
omitted, the whole story becomes an enigma, and we are
often tempted to substitute some less creditable explanation of errors for the true one. We should not do justice
to Johnson's intense tenderness, if we did not see how
often it was masked by an irritability pardonable in itself,
and not affecting the deeper springs of action. To bring
out the beauty of a character by means of its external
oddities is the triumph of a kindly humourist; and Boswell would have acted as absurdly in suppressing Johnson's
weaknesses, as Sterne would have done had he made Uncle
Toby a perfectly sound and rational person. But to see
this required an insight so rare that it is wanting in nearly

all the biographers who have followed Boswell's steps,
and is the most conclusive proof that Boswell was a man
of a higher intellectual capacity than has been generally
admitted.

CHAPTER IV.

JOHNSON AS A LITERARY DICTATOR.

WE have now reached the point at which Johnson's life becomes distinctly visible through the eyes of a competent observer. The last twenty years are those which are really familiar to us ; and little remains but to give some brief selection of Boswell's anecdotes. The task, however, is a difficult one. It is easy enough to make a selection of the gems of Boswell's narrative ; but it is also inevitable that, taken from their setting, they should lose the greatest part of their brilliance. We lose all the quaint semi-conscious touches of character which make the original so fascinating ; and Boswell's absurdities become less amusing when we are able to forget for an instant that the perpetrator is also the narrator. The effort, however, must be made ; and it will be best to premise a brief statement of the external conditions of the life.

From the time of the pension until his death, Johnson was elevated above the fear of poverty. He had a pleasant refuge at the Thrales', where much of his time was spent ; and many friends gathered round him and regarded his utterances with even excessive admiration. He had still frequent periods of profound depression. His diaries reveal an inner life tormented by gloomy forebodings, by remorse for past indolence and futile resolutions of amendment ; but he could always escape from himself to a society of friends and admirers. His abandonment of wine seems to have improved his health and diminished the intensity of his melancholy fits. His literary activity, however, nearly ceased. He wrote a few political pamphlets in defence of Government, and after a long period of indolence managed to complete his last conspicuous work—the *Lives of the Poets*, which was published in 1779 and 1781. One other book of some interest appeared in 1775. It was an account of the journey made with Boswell to the Hebrides in 1773. This journey was in fact the chief interruption to the even tenour of his life. He made a tour to Wales with the Thrales in 1774 ; and spent a month with them in Paris in 1775. For the rest of the period he lived chiefly in London or at Streatham, making occasional trips to Lichfield and Oxford, or paying visits to Taylor, Langton, and one or two other friends. It was, however, in the London which he loved so ardently ("a man," he said once, "who is tired of London is tired of life"), that he was chiefly conspicuous. There he talked and drank tea illimitably at his friends' houses, or argued and laid down the law to his disciples collected in a tavern instead of Academic groves. Especially he was in all his glory at the Club, which began its meetings in February, 1764, and was afterwards known as the Literary Club. This Club was founded by Sir Joshua Reynolds, "our Romulus," as Johnson called him. The original members were Reynolds, Johnson, Burke, Nugent, Beauclerk, Langton, Goldsmith, Chamier, and Hawkins. They met weekly at the Turk's Head, in Gerard Street, Soho, at seven o'clock, and the talk generally continued till a late hour. The Club was afterwards increased in numbers, and the weekly supper changed to a fortnightly dinner. It continued to thrive, and election to it came to be as great an honour in certain

circles as election to a membership of Parliament. Among
the members elected in Johnson's lifetime were Percy of
the *Reliques*, Garrick, Sir W. Jones, Boswell, Fox, Stee-
vens, Gibbon, Adam Smith, the Wartons, Sheridan, Dun-
ning, Sir Joseph Banks, Windham, Lord Stowell, Malone,
and Dr. Burney. What was best in the conversation at
the time was doubtless to be found at its meetings.

Johnson's habitual mode of life is described by Dr.
Maxwell, one of Boswell's friends, who made his acquaintance in 1754. Maxwell generally called upon him about
twelve, and found him in bed or declaiming over his tea.
A levée, chiefly of literary men, surrounded him; and he
seemed to be regarded as a kind of oracle to whom every
one might resort for advice or instruction. After talking
all the morning, he dined at a tavern, staying late and
then going to some friend's house for tea, over which he
again loitered for a long time. Maxwell is puzzled to
know when he could have read or written. The answer
seems to be pretty obvious; namely, that after the publication of the *Dictionary* he wrote very little, and that,
when he did write, it was generally in a brief spasm of
feverish energy. One may understand that Johnson should
have frequently reproached himself for his indolence;
though he seems to have occasionally comforted himself
by thinking that he could do good by talking as well as
by writing. He said that a man should have a part of his
life to himself; and compared himself to a physician retired to a small town from practice in a great city. Boswell, in spite of this, said that he still wondered that
Johnson had not more pleasure in writing than in not
writing. " Sir," replied the oracle, " you *may* wonder."

I will now endeavour, with Boswell's guidance, to describe a few of the characteristic scenes which can be fully

H

enjoyed in his pages alone.   The first must be the introduction of Boswell to the sage.   Boswell had come to
London eager for the acquaintance of literary magnates.
He already knew Goldsmith, who had inflamed his desire
for an introduction to Johnson.   Once when Boswell spoke
of Levett, one of Johnson's dependents, Goldsmith had said,
"he is poor and honest, which is recommendation enough
to Johnson." Another time, when Boswell had wondered
at Johnson's kindness to a man of bad character, Goldsmith had replied, " He is now become miserable, and that
insures the protection of Johnson."   Boswell had hoped
for an introduction through the elder Sheridan ; but
Sheridan never forgot the contemptuous phrase in which
Johnson had referred to his fellow-pensioner.   Possibly
Sheridan had heard of one other Johnsonian remark.
" Why, sir," he had said, " Sherry is dull, naturally dull ;
but it must have taken him a great deal of pains to become what we now see him.   Such an excess of stupidity,
sir, is not in Nature."   At another time he said, " Sheridan cannot bear me ; I bring his declamation to a point."
" What influence can Mr. Sheridan have upon the language of this great country by his narrow exertions ?   Sir,
it is burning a farthing candle at Dover to show light at
Calais."   Boswell, however, was acquainted with Davies,
an actor turned bookseller, now chiefly remembered by a
line in Churchill's *Rosciad* which is said to have driven
him from the stage—

> He mouths a sentence as curs mouth a bone.

Boswell was drinking tea with Davies and his wife in their
back parlour when Johnson came into the shop.   Davies,
seeing him through the glass-door, announced his approach
to Boswell in the spirit of Horatio addressing Hamlet :

"Look, my Lord, it comes!" Davies introduced the
young Scotchman, who remembered Johnson's proverbial
prejudices. "Don't tell him where I come from!" cried
Boswell. "From Scotland," said Davies roguishly. "Mr.
Johnson," said Boswell, "I do indeed come from Scotland ; but I cannot help it!" "That, sir," was the first of
Johnson's many retorts to his worshipper, "is what a great
many of your countrymen cannot help."

Poor Boswell was stunned; but he recovered when
Johnson observed to Davies, "What do you think of Garrick? He has refused me an order for the play for Miss
Williams because he knows the house will be full, and
that an order would be worth three shillings." "O, sir,"
intruded the unlucky Boswell, "I cannot think Mr. Garrick would grudge such a trifle to you." "Sir," replied
Johnson sternly, "I have known David Garrick longer
than you have done, and I know no right you have to
talk to me on the subject." The second blow might have
crushed a less intrepid curiosity. Boswell, though silenced,
gradually recovered sufficiently to listen, and afterwards
to note down parts of the conversation. As the interview
went on, he even ventured to make a remark or two, which
were very civilly received ; Davies consoled him at his
departure by assuring him that the great man liked him
very well. "I cannot conceive a more humiliating position," said Beauclerk on another occasion, "than to be
clapped on the back by Tom Davies." For the present,
however, even Tom Davies was a welcome encourager to
one who, for the rest, was not easily rebuffed. A few
days afterwards Boswell ventured a call, was kindly received and detained for some time by "the giant in his
den." He was still a little afraid of the said giant, who
had shortly before administered a vigorous retort to his

countryman Blair. Blair had asked Johnson whether he thought that any man of a modern age could have written *Ossian.* "Yes, sir," replied Johnson, "many men, many women, and many children." Boswell, however, got on very well, and before long had the high honour of drinking a bottle of port with Johnson at the Mitre, and receiving, after a little autobiographical sketch, the emphatic approval, "Give me your hand, I have taken a liking to you."

In a very short time Boswell was on sufficiently easy terms with Johnson, not merely to frequent his levées but to ask him to dinner at the Mitre. He gathered up, though without the skill of his later performances, some fragments of the conversational feast. The great man aimed another blow or two at Scotch prejudices. To an unlucky compatriot of Boswell's, who claimed for his country a great many "noble wild prospects," Johnson replied, "I believe, sir, you have a great many, Norway, too, has noble wild prospects; and Lapland is remarkable for prodigious noble wild prospects. But, sir, let me tell you the noblest prospect which a Scotchman ever sees, is the high road that leads him to England." Though Boswell makes a slight remonstrance about the "rude grandeur of Nature" as seen in "Caledonia," he sympathized in this with his teacher. Johnson said afterwards, that he never knew any one with "such a gust for London." Before long he was trying Boswell's tastes by asking him in Greenwich Park, "Is not this very fine?" "Yes, sir," replied the promising disciple, "but not equal to Fleet Street." "You are right, sir," said the sage; and Boswell illustrates his dictum by the authority of a "very fashionable baronet," and, moreover, a baronet from Rydal, who declared that the fragrance of a May evening in the country might be very well, but

that he preferred the smell of a flambeau at the playhouse.
In more serious moods Johnson delighted his new disciple
by discussions upon theological, social, and literary topics.
He argued with an unfortunate friend of Boswell's, whose
mind, it appears, had been poisoned by Hume, and who
was, moreover, rash enough to undertake the defence of
principles of political equality. Johnson's view of all
propagators of new opinions was tolerably simple. " Hume,
and other sceptical innovators," he said, " are vain men,
and will gratify themselves at any expense. Truth will
not afford sufficient food to their vanity ; so they have
betaken themselves to error. Truth, sir, is a cow which
will yield such people no more milk, and so they are gone
to milk the bull." On another occasion poor Boswell,
not yet acquainted with the master's prejudices, quoted
with hearty laughter a " very strange " story which Hume
had told him of Johnson. According to Hume, Johnson
had said that he would stand before a battery of cannon
to restore Convocation to its full powers. " And would I
not, sir ?" thundered out the sage with flashing eyes and
threatening gestures. Boswell judiciously bowed to the
storm, and diverted Johnson's attention. Another mani-
festation of orthodox prejudice was less terrible. Boswell
told Johnson that he had heard a Quaker woman preach.
" A woman's preaching," said Johnson, " is like a dog's
walking on his hind legs. It is not done well ; but you
are surprised to find it done at all."

So friendly had the pair become, that when Boswell left
England to continue his studies at Utrecht, Johnson accompanied him in the stage-coach to Harwich, amusing him
on the way by his frankness of address to fellow-passen-
gers, and by the voracity of his appetite. He gave him
some excellent advice, remarking of a moth which flut-

tered into a candle, "that creature was its own tormentor, and I believe its name was Boswell." He refuted Berkeley by striking his foot with mighty force against a large stone, till he rebounded from it. As the ship put out to sea Boswell watched him from the deck, whilst he remained "rolling his majestic frame in his usual manner." And so the friendship was cemented, though Boswell disappeared for a time from the scene, travelled on the Continent, and visited Paoli in Corsica. A friendly letter or two kept up the connexion till Boswell returned in 1766, with his head full of Corsica and a projected book of travels.

In the next year, 1767, occurred an incident upon which Boswell dwells with extreme complacency. Johnson was in the habit of sometimes reading in the King's Library, and it came into the head of his majesty that he should like to see the uncouth monster upon whom he had bestowed a pension. In spite of his semi-humorous Jacobitism, there was probably not a more loyal subject in his majesty's dominions. Loyalty is a word too often used to designate a sentiment worthy only of valets, advertising tradesmen, and writers of claptrap articles. But it deserves all respect when it reposes, as in Johnson's case, upon a profound conviction of the value of political subordination, and an acceptance of the king as the authorized representative of a great principle. There was no touch of servility in Johnson's respect for his sovereign, a respect fully reconcilable with a sense of his own personal dignity. Johnson spoke of his interview with an unfeigned satisfaction, which it would be difficult in these days to preserve from the taint of snobbishness. He described it frequently to his friends, and Boswell with pious care ascertained the details from Johnson himself, and from various secondary sources. He contrived afterwards to get his minute submitted to the King himself, who graciously authorized its publication. When he was preparing his biography, he published this account with the letter to Chesterfield in a small pamphlet sold at a prohibitory price, in order to secure the copyright.

"I find," said Johnson afterwards, "that it does a man good to be talked to by his sovereign. In the first place a man cannot be in a passion." What other advantages he perceived must be unknown, for here the oracle was interrupted. But whatever the advantages, it could hardly be reckoned amongst them, that there would be room for the hearty cut and thrust retorts which enlivened his ordinary talk. To us accordingly the conversation is chiefly interesting as illustrating what Johnson meant by his politeness. He found that the King wanted him to talk, and he talked accordingly. He spoke in a "firm manly manner, with a sonorous voice," and not in the subdued tone customary at formal receptions. He dilated upon various literary topics, on the libraries of Oxford and Cambridge, on some contemporary controversies, on the quack Dr. Hill, and upon the reviews of the day. All that is worth repeating is a complimentary passage which shows Johnson's possession of that courtesy which rests upon sense and self-respect. The King asked whether he was writing anything, and Johnson excused himself by saying that he had told the world what he knew for the present, and had "done his part as a writer." "I should have thought so too," said the King, "if you had not written so well." "No man," said Johnson, "could have paid a higher compliment ; and it was fit for a King to pay—it was decisive." When asked if he had replied, he said, "No, sir. When the King had said it, it was to be. It was not for me to bandy civilities with my sovereign."

Johnson was not the less delighted. "Sir," he said to the librarian, "they may talk of the King as they will, but he is the finest gentleman I have ever seen." And he afterwards compared his manners to those of Louis XIV., and his favourite, Charles II. Goldsmith, says Boswell, was silent during the narrative, because (so his kind friend supposed) he was jealous of the honour paid to the dictator. But his natural simplicity prevailed. He ran to Johnson, and exclaimed in 'a kind of flutter,' "Well, you acquitted yourself in this conversation better than I should have done, for I should have bowed and stammered through the whole of it."

The years 1768 and 1769 were a period of great excitement for Boswell. He was carrying on various love affairs, which ended with his marriage in the end of 1769. He was publishing his book upon Corsica and paying homage to Paoli, who arrived in England in the autumn of the same year. The book appeared in the beginning of 1768, and he begs his friend Temple to report all that is said about it, but with the restriction that he is to conceal *all censure*. He particularly wanted Gray's opinion, as Gray was a friend of Temple's. Gray's opinion, not conveyed to Boswell, was expressed by his calling it "a dialogue between a green goose and a hero." Boswell, who was cultivating the society of various eminent people, exclaims triumphantly in a letter to Temple (April 26, 1768), "I am really the great man now." Johnson and Hume had called upon him on the same day, and Garrick, Franklin, and Oglethorpe also partook of his "admirable dinners and good claret." "This," he says, with the sense that he deserved his honours, "is enjoying the fruit of my labours, and appearing like the friend of Paoli." Johnson in vain expressed a wish that he would "empty his head of

Corsica, which had filled it too long."   "Empty my head
of Corsica !   Empty it of honour, empty it of friendship,
empty it of piety !" exclaims the ardent youth.   The next
year accordingly saw Boswell's appearance at the Stratford
Jubilee, where he paraded to the admiration of all beholders
in a costume described by himself (apparently) in a glow-
ing article in the *London Magazine*.   " Is it wrong, sir,"
he took speedy opportunity of inquiring from the oracle,
" to affect singularity in order to make people stare ? "
" Yes," replied Johnson, "if you do it by propagating
error, and indeed it is wrong in any way.   There is in
human nature a general inclination to make people stare,
and every wise man has himself to cure of it, and does
cure himself.   If you wish to make people stare by doing
better than others, why make them stare till they stare
their eyes out.   But consider how easy it is to make
people stare by being absurd "—a proposition which he
proceeds to illustrate by examples perhaps less telling than
Boswell's recent performance.

The sage was less communicative on the question of
marriage, though Boswell had anticipated some " instructive conversation " upon that topic.   His sole remark was
one from which Boswell " humbly differed."   Johnson
maintained that a wife was not the worse for being
learned.   Boswell, on the other hand, defined the proper
degree of intelligence to be desired in a female companion
by some verses in which Sir Thomas Overbury says that
a wife should have some knowledge, and be " by nature
wise, not learned much by art."   Johnson said afterwards
that Mrs. Boswell was in a proper degree inferior to her
husband.   So far as we can tell, she seems to have
been a really sensible and good woman, who kept her
husband's absurdities in check, and was, in her way,

a better wife than he deserved. So, happily, are most wives.

Johnson and Boswell had several meetings in 1769. Boswell had the honour of introducing the two objects of his idolatry, Johnson and Paoli, and on another occasion entertained a party including Goldsmith and Garrick and Reynolds, at his lodgings in Old Bond Street. We can still see the meeting more distinctly than many that have been swallowed by a few days of oblivion. They waited for one of the party, Johnson kindly maintaining that six ought to be kept waiting for one, if the one would suffer more by the others sitting down than the six by waiting. Meanwhile Garrick " played round Johnson with a fond vivacity, taking hold of the breasts of his coat, looking up in his face with a lively archness," and complimenting him on his good health. Goldsmith strutted about bragging of his dress, of which Boswell, in the serene consciousness of superiority to such weakness, thought him seriously vain. " Let me tell you," said Goldsmith, " when my tailor brought home my bloom-coloured coat, he said, ' Sir, I have a favour to beg of you; when anybody asks you who made your clothes, be pleased to mention John Filby, at the Harrow, Water Lane.' " " Why, sir," said Johnson, " that was because he knew that the strange colour would attract crowds to gaze at it, and thus they might hear of him, and see how well he could make a coat even of so absurd a colour." Mr. Filby has gone the way of all tailors and bloom-coloured coats, but some of his bills are preserved. On the day of this dinner he had delivered to Goldsmith a half-dress suit of ratteen lined with satin, costing twelve guineas, a pair of silk stocking-breeches for £2 5s. and a pair of bloom-coloured ditto for £1 4s. 6d. The bill, including other items, was paid, it is satisfactory to add, in February, 1771.

The conversation was chiefly literary. Johnson repeated the concluding lines of the *Dunciad;* upon which some one (probably Boswell) ventured to say that they were " too fine for such a poem—a poem on what ? "   " Why," said Johnson, " on dunces !   It was worth while being a dunce then.   Ah, sir, hadst *thou* lived in those days ! " Johnson presently uttered a criticism which has led some people to think that he had a touch of the dunce in him.   He declared that a description of a temple in Congreve's *Mourning Bride* was the finest he knew— finer than anything in Shakspeare.   Garrick vainly protested; but Johnson was inexorable.   He compared Congreve to a man who had only ten guineas in the world, but all in one coin; whereas Shakspeare might have ten thousand separate guineas.   The principle of the criticism is rather curious.   " What I mean is," said Johnson, " that you can show me no passage where there is simply a description of material objects, without any admixture of moral notions, which produces such an effect."   The description of the night before Agincourt was rejected because there were men in it; and the description of Dover Cliff because the boats and the crows " impede yon fall."   They do " not impress your mind at once with the horrible idea of immense height.   The impression is divided; you pass on by computation from one stage of the tremendous space to another."

Probably most people will think that the passage in question deserves a very slight fraction of the praise bestowed upon it; but the criticism, like most of Johnson's, has a meaning which might be worth examining abstractedly from the special application which shocks the

idolaters of Shakspeare. Presently the party discussed
Mrs. Montagu, whose Essay upon Shakspeare had made
some noise. Johnson had a respect for her, caused in
great measure by a sense of her liberality to his friend Miss
Williams, of whom more must be said hereafter. He
paid her some tremendous compliments, observing that
some China plates which had belonged to Queen Elizabeth
and to her, had no reason to be ashamed of a possessor so
little inferior to the first. But he had his usual professional contempt for her amateur performances in literature.
Her defence of Shakspeare against Voltaire did her honour,
he admitted, but it would do nobody else honour. " No,
sir, there is no real criticism in it : none showing the
beauty of thought, as formed on the workings of the human
heart." Mrs. Montagu was reported once to have com-
plimented a modern tragedian, probably Jephson, by saying, "I tremble for Shakspeare." "When Shakspeare," said
Johnson, "has got Jephson for his rival and Mrs. Montagu
for his defender, he is in a poor state indeed." The conversation went on to a recently published book, *Kames's
Elements of Criticism,* which Johnson praised, whilst Goldsmith said more truly, " It is easier to write that book than
to read it." Johnson went on to speak of other critics.
" There is no great merit," he said, " in telling how many
plays have ghosts in them, and how this ghost is better
than that. You must show how terror is impressed on the
human heart. In the description of night in *Macbeth* the
beetle and the bat detract from the general idea of dark-
ness—inspissated gloom."

After Boswell's marriage he disappeared for some
time from London, and his correspondence with Johnson
dropped, as he says, without coldness, from pure procras-
tination. He did not return to London till 1772. In the

spring of that and the following year he renewed his old
habits of intimacy, and inquired into Johnson's opinion upon
various subjects ranging from ghosts to literary criticism.
The height to which he had risen in the doctor's good
opinion was marked by several symptoms. He was asked
to dine at Johnson's house upon Easter day, 1773; and
observes that his curiosity was as much gratified as by a
previous dinner with Rousseau in the "wilds of Neuf-
chatel." He was now able to report, to the amazement of
many inquirers, that Johnson's establishment was quite
orderly. The meal consisted of very good soup, a boiled
leg of lamb with spinach, a veal pie, and a rice pudding.
A stronger testimony of good-will was his election, by
Johnson's influence, into the Club. It ought apparently
to be said that Johnson forced him upon the Club by
letting it be understood that, till Boswell was admitted,
no other candidate would have a chance. Boswell, however, was, as his proposer said, a thoroughly "clubable"
man, and once a member, his good humour secured his
popularity. On the important evening Boswell dined at
Beauclerk's with his proposer and some other members.
The talk turned upon Goldsmith's merits; and Johnson
not only defended his poetry, but preferred him as a historian to Robertson. Such a judgment could be explained
in Boswell's opinion by nothing but Johnson's dislike to
the Scotch. Once before, when Boswell had mentioned
Robertson in order to meet Johnson's condemnation of
Scotch literature in general, Johnson had evaded him;
" Sir, I love Robertson, and I won't talk of his book." On
the present occasion he said that he would give to Robertson the advice offered by an old college tutor to a pupil;
" read over your compositions, and whenever you meet with
a passage which you think particularly fine, strike it out."

A good anecdote of Goldsmith followed. Johnson had said to him once in the Poets' Corner at Westminster,—

Forsitan et nostrum nomen miscebitur istis.

When they got to Temple Bar Goldsmith pointed to the heads of the Jacobites upon it and slily suggested,—

Forsitan et nostrum nomen miscebitur *istis*.

Johnson next pronounced a critical judgment which should be set against many sins of that kind. He praised the *Pilgrim's Progress* very warmly, and suggested that Bunyan had probably read Spenser.

After more talk the gentlemen went to the Club; and poor Boswell remained trembling with an anxiety which even the claims of Lady Di Beauclerk's conversation could not dissipate. The welcome news of his election was brought; and Boswell went to see Burke for the first time, and to receive a humorous charge from Johnson, pointing out the conduct expected from him as a good member. Perhaps some hints were given as to betrayal of confidence. Boswell seems at any rate to have had a certain reserve in repeating Club talk.

This intimacy with Johnson was about to receive a more public and even more impressive stamp. The antipathy to Scotland and the Scotch already noticed was one of Johnson's most notorious crotchets. The origin of the prejudice was forgotten by Johnson himself, though he was willing to accept a theory started by old Sheridan that it was resentment for the betrayal of Charles I. There is, however, nothing surprising in Johnson's partaking a prejudice common enough from the days of his youth, when each people supposed itself to have been cheated by the

Union, and Englishmen resented the advent of swarms of
needy adventurers, talking with a strange accent and hanging together with honourable but vexatious persistence.
Johnson was irritated by what was, after all, a natural defence against English prejudice.   He declared that the
Scotch were always ready to lie on each other's behalf.
" The Irish," he said, " are not in a conspiracy to cheat the
world by false representations of the merits of their countrymen.   No, sir, the Irish are a fair people ; they never speak
well of one another."   There was another difference.   He
always expressed a generous resentment against the tyranny
exercised by English rulers over the Irish people.   To some
one who defended the restriction of Irish trade for the
good of English merchants, he said, " Sir, you talk the
language of a savage.   What ! sir, would you prevent any
people from feeding themselves, if by any honest means
they can do it ? "   It was " better to hang or drown people
at once," than weaken them by unrelenting persecution.
He felt some tenderness for Catholics, especially when
oppressed, and a hearty antipathy towards prosperous Pres-
byterians.   The Lowland Scotch were typified by John
Knox, in regard to whom he expressed a hope, after view-
ing the ruins of St. Andrew's, that he was buried " in the
highway."

This sturdy British and High Church prejudice did not
prevent the worthy doctor from having many warm friendships with Scotchmen, and helping many distressed Scotchmen in London.   Most of the amanuenses employed for
his *Dictionary* were Scotch.   But he nourished the prejudice the more as giving an excellent pretext for many
keen gibes.   " Scotch learning," he said, for example, " is
like bread in a besieged town.   Every man gets a mouth-
ful, but no man a bellyful."   Once Strahan said in an-

swer to some abusive remarks, "Well, sir, God made
Scotland." "Certainly," replied Johnson, "but we must
always remember that He made it for Scotchmen; and
comparisons are odious, Mr. Strahan, but God made hell."

Boswell, therefore, had reason to feel both triumph and
alarm when he induced the great man to accompany him
in a Scotch tour. Boswell's journal of the tour appeared
soon after Johnson's death. Johnson himself wrote an
account of it, which is not without interest, though it is
in his dignified style, which does not condescend to Boswellian touches of character. In 1773 the Scotch High-
lands were still a little known region, justifying a book
descriptive of manners and customs, and touching upon
antiquities now the commonplaces of innumerable guide
books. Scott was still an infant, and the day of enthusiasm, real or affected, for mountain scenery had not yet
dawned. Neither of the travellers, as Boswell remarks,
cared much for "rural beauties." Johnson says quaintly
on the shores of Loch Ness, "It will very readily occur
that this uniformity of barrenness can afford very little
amusement to the traveller; that it is easy to sit at home
and conceive rocks and heath and waterfalls; and that
these journeys are useless labours, which neither impreg-
nate the imagination nor enlarge the understanding." And
though he shortly afterwards sits down on a bank "such
as a writer of romance might have delighted to feign," and
there conceived the thought of his book, he does not seem
to have felt much enthusiasm. He checked Boswell for
describing a hill as "immense," and told him that it was
only a "considerable protuberance." Indeed it is not
surprising if he sometimes grew weary in long rides upon
Highland ponies, or if, when weatherbound in a remote vil-
lage in Skye, he declared that this was a "waste of life."

On the whole, however, Johnson bore his fatigues well,
preserved his temper, and made sensible remarks upon
men and things. The pair started from Edinburgh in
the middle of August, 1773 ; they went north along the
eastern coast, through St. Andrew's, Aberdeen, Banff,
Fort George, and Inverness. There they took to horses,
rode to Glenelg, and took boat for Skye, where they landed
on the 2nd of September. They visited Raasay, Coll,
Mull, and Iona, and after some dangerous sailing got to
the mainland at Oban on October 2nd. Thence they proceeded by Inverary and Loch Lomond to Glasgow ; and
after paying a visit to Boswell's paternal mansion at
Auchinleck in Ayrshire, returned to Edinburgh in November. It were too long to narrate their adventures at
length, or to describe in detail how Johnson grieved over
traces of the iconoclastic zeal of Knox's disciples, seriously investigated stories of second-sight, cross-examined
and brow-beat credulous believers in the authenticity of
Ossian, and felt his piety grow warm among the ruins
of Iona. Once or twice, when the temper of the travellers
was tried by the various worries incident to their position,
poor Boswell came in for some severe blows. But he
was happy, feeling, as he remarks, like a dog who has run
away with a large piece of meat, and is devouring it
peacefully in a corner by himself. Boswell's spirits were
irrepressible. On hearing a drum beat for dinner at
Fort George, he says, with a Pepys-like touch, " I for a
little while fancied myself a military man, and it pleased
me." He got scandalously drunk on one occasion, and
showed reprehensible levity on others. He bored Johnson
by inquiring too curiously into his reasons for not wearing a nightcap—a subject which seems to have interested
him profoundly ; he permitted himself to say in his

I

journal that he was so much pleased with some pretty
ladies' maids at the Duke of Argyll's, that he felt he could
"have been a knight-errant for them," and his "venerable
fellow-traveller" read the passage without censuring his
levity.   The great man himself could be equally volatile.
" I *have often thought*," he observed one day, to Boswell's
amusement, " that if I kept a seraglio, the ladies should
all wear linen gowns "—as more cleanly.   The pair agreed
in trying to stimulate the feudal zeal of various Highland
chiefs with whom they came in contact, and who were
unreasonable enough to show a hankering after the luxuries
of civilization.

Though Johnson seems to have been generally on his
best behaviour, he had a rough encounter or two with
some of the more civilized natives.   Boswell piloted him
safely through a visit to Lord Monboddo, a man of real
ability, though the proprietor of crochets as eccentric as
Johnson's, and consequently divided from him by strong
mutual prejudices.   At Auchinleck he was less fortunate.
The old laird, who was the staunchest of Whigs, had not
relished his son's hero-worship.   "There is nae hope for
Jamie, mon ; Jamie is gaen clean gyte.   What do you
think, mon ?   He's done wi' Paoli—he's off wi' the land-
louping scoundrel of a Corsican, and who's tail do you
think he's pinned himself to now, mon?"   "Here," says
Sir Walter Scott, the authority for the story, "the old
judge summoned up a sneer of most sovereign contempt.
'A dominie, mon—an auld dominie—he keeped a schŭle
and caauld it an acaademy.'"   The two managed to
keep the peace till, one day during Johnson's visit,
they got upon Oliver Cromwell.   Boswell suppresses
the scene with obvious reluctance, his openness being
checked for once by filial respect.   Scott has fortu-

nately preserved the climax˙ of old Boswell's argument.
"What had Cromwell done for his country?" asked
Johnson.   " God, doctor, he gart Kings ken that they
had a *lith* in their necks" retorted the laird, in a
phrase worthy of Mr. Carlyle himself.   Scott reports one
other scene, at which respectable commentators, like
Croker, hold up their hands in horror.   Should we regret
or rejoice to say that it involves an obvious inaccuracy?
The authority, however, is too good to allow us to suppose
that it was without some foundation.   Adam Smith, it is
said, met Johnson at Glasgow and had an altercation with
him about the well-known account of Hume's death.   As
Hume did not die till three years later, there must be
some error in this.   The dispute, however, whatever its
date or subject, ended by Johnson saying to Smith, " *You
lie.*"   " And what did you reply?" was asked of Smith.
" I said, 'you are a son of a ——.'"   " On such terms,"
says Scott, "did these two great moralists meet and part,
and such was the classical dialogue between these two
great teachers of morality."

   In the year 1774 Boswell found it expedient to atone
for his long absence in the previous year by staying at
home.   Johnson managed to complete his account of the
Scotch Tour, which was published at the end of the year.
Among other consequences was a violent controversy
with the lovers of *Ossian*.   Johnson was a thorough sceptic as to the authenticity of the book.   His scepticism
did not repose upon the philological or antiquarian reason-
ings, which would be applicable in the controversy from
internal evidence.   It was to some extent the expression of
a general incredulity which astonished his friends, especially when contrasted with his tenderness for many puerile
superstitions.   He could scarcely be induced to admit the

truth of any narrative which struck him as odd, and it
was long, for example, before he would believe even in the
Lisbon earthquake. Yet he seriously discussed the truth
of second-sight ; he carefully investigated the Cock-lane
ghost—a goblin who anticipated some of the modern phe-
nomena of so-called " spiritualism," and with almost equal
absurdity ; he told stories to Boswell about a " shadowy
being" which had once been seen by Cave, and declared
that he had once heard his mother call " Sam " when he
was at Oxford and she at Lichfield. The apparent incon-
sistency was in truth natural enough. Any man who
clings with unreasonable pertinacity to the prejudices of
his childhood, must be alternately credulous and sceptical
in excess. In both cases, he judges by his fancies in defiance of evidence ; and accepts and rejects according to
his likes and dislikes, instead of his estimates of logical
proof. *Ossian* would be naturally offensive to Johnson,
as one of the earliest and most remarkable manifestations
of that growing taste for what was called " Nature," as
opposed to civilization, of which Rousseau was the great
mouthpiece. Nobody more heartily despised this form of
" cant " than Johnson. A man who utterly despised the
scenery of the Hebrides as compared with Greenwich
Park or Charing Cross, would hardly take kindly to the
Ossianesque version of the mountain passion. The book
struck him as sheer rubbish. I have already quoted
the retort about " many men, many women, and many
children." " A man," he said, on another occasion,
" might write such stuff for ever, if he would abandon his
mind to it."

The precise point, however, upon which he rested his
case, was the tangible one of the inability of Macpherson
to produce the manuscripts of which he had affirmed the

existence. Macpherson wrote a furious letter to Johnson, of which the purport can only be inferred from Johnson's smashing retort,—

" Mr. James MacPherson, I have received your foolish and impudent letter. Any violence offered me I shall do my best to repel; and what I cannot do for myself, the law shall do for me. I hope I shall never be deterred from detecting what I think a cheat by the menaces of a ruffian.

" What would you have me retract? I thought your book an imposture : I think it an imposture still. For this opinion I have given my reasons to the public, which I here dare you to refute. Your rage I defy. Your abilities, since your *Homer*, are not so formidable ; and what I hear of your morals inclines me to pay regard not to what you shall say, but to what you shall prove. You may print this if you will.

" Sam. Johnson."

And so laying in a tremendous cudgel, the old gentleman (he was now sixty-six) awaited the assault, which, however, was not delivered.

In 1775 Boswell again came to London, and renewed some of the Scotch discussions. He attended a meeting of the Literary Club, and found the members disposed to laugh at Johnson's tenderness to the stories about second-sight. Boswell heroically avowed his own belief. " The evidence," he said, " is enough for me, though not for his great mind. What will not fill a quart bottle, will fill a pint bottle. I am filled with belief." " Are you ?" said Colman ; " then cork it up."

It was during this and the next few years that Boswell laboured most successfully in gathering materials for his book. In 1777 he only met Johnson in the country. In

1779, for some unexplained reason, he was lazy in making notes ; in 1780 and 1781 he was absent from London ; and in the following year, Johnson was visibly declining. The tenour of Johnson's life was interrupted during this period by no remarkable incidents, and his literary activity was not great, although the composition of the *Lives of the Poets* falls between 1777 and 1780. His mind, however, as represented by his talk, was in full vigour. I will take in order of time a few of the passages recorded by Boswell, which may serve for various reasons to afford the best illustration of his character. Yet it may be worth while once more to repeat the warning that such fragments moved from their context must lose most of their charm.

On March 26th (1775), Boswell met Johnson at the house of the publisher, Strahan. Strahan reminded John-son of a characteristic remark which he had formerly made, that there are " few ways in which a man can be more innocently employed than in getting money." On another occasion Johnson observed with equal truth, if less originality, that cultivating kindness was an important part of life, as well as money-making. Johnson then asked to see a country lad whom he had recommended to Strahan as an apprentice. He asked for five guineas on account, that he might give one to the boy. " Nay, if a man recommends a boy and does nothing for him, it is sad work." A " little, thick short-legged boy " was accord-ingly brought into the courtyard, whither Johnson and Boswell descended, and the lexicographer bending him-self down administered some good advice to the awe-struck lad with " slow and sonorous solemnity," ending by the presentation of the guinea.

In the evening the pair formed part of a corps of party

" wits," led by Sir Joshua Reynolds, to the benefit of Mrs. Abingdon, who had been a frequent model of the painter. Johnson praised Garrick's prologues, and Boswell kindly reported the eulogy to Garrick, with whom he supped at Beauclerk's. Garrick treated him to a mimicry of Johnson, repeating, " with pauses and half-whistling," the lines,—

> Os homini sublime dedit—cœlumque tueri
> Jussit—et erectos ad sidera tollere vultus :

looking downwards, and at the end touching the ground with a contorted gesticulation. Garrick was generally jealous of Johnson's light opinion of him, and used to take off his old master, saying, " Davy has some convivial pleasantry about him, but 'tis a futile fellow."

Next day, at Thrales', Johnson fell foul of Gray, one of his pet aversions. Boswell denied that Gray was dull in poetry. " Sir," replied Johnson, " he was dull in company, dull in his closet, dull everywhere. He was dull in a new way, and that made people think him great. He was a mechanical poet." He proceeded to say that there were only two good stanzas in the *Elegy*. Johnson's criticism was perverse; but if we were to collect a few of the judgments passed by contemporaries upon each other, it would be scarcely exceptional in its want of appreciation. It is rather odd to remark that Gray was generally condemned for obscurity—a charge which seems strangely out of place when he is measured by more recent standards.

A day or two afterwards some one rallied Johnson on his appearance at Mrs. Abingdon's benefit. " Why did you go ? " he asked. " Did you see ? "   " No, sir." " Did you hear ? "   " No, sir."   " Why, then, sir, did you

go ? " " Because, sir, she is a favourite of the public ;
and when the public cares the thousandth part for you
that it does for her, I will go to your benefit too."

The day after, Boswell won a bet from Lady Di
Beauclerk by venturing to ask Johnson what he did with
the orange-peel which he used to pocket.   Johnson
received the question amicably, but did not clear the
mystery.   "Then," said Boswell, " the world must be
left in the dark.   It must be said, he scraped them,
and he let them dry, but what he did with them next he
never could be prevailed upon to tell."   " Nay, sir,"
replied Johnson, " you should say it more emphatically—
he could not be prevailed upon, even by his dearest
friends to tell."

This year Johnson received the degree of LL.D. from
Oxford.   He had previously (in 1765) received the same
honour from Dublin.   It is remarkable, however, that
familiar as the title has become, Johnson called himself
plain Mr. to the end of his days, and was generally so
called by his intimates.   On April 2nd, at a dinner at
Hoole's, Johnson made another assault upon Gray and
Mason.   When Boswell said that there were good passages
in Mason's *Elfrida*, he conceded that there were " now and
then some good imitations of Milton's bad manner."   After
some more talk, Boswell spoke of the cheerfulness of Fleet
Street.   " Why, sir," said Johnson, " Fleet Street has a
very animated appearance, but I think that the full tide
of human existence is at Charing Cross."   He added a
story of an eminent tallow-chandler who had made a fortune in London, and was foolish enough to retire to the
country.   He grew so tired of his retreat, that he begged
to know the melting-days of his successor, that he might
be present at the operation.

On April 7th, they dined at a tavern, where the talk turned upon *Ossian*. Some one mentioned as an objection to its authenticity that no mention of wolves occurred in it. Johnson fell into a reverie upon wild beasts, and, whilst Reynolds and Langton were discussing something, he broke out, "Pennant tells of bears." What Pennant told is unknown. The company continued to talk, whilst Johnson continued his monologue, the word "bear" occurring at intervals, like a word in a catch. At last, when a pause came, he was going on : "We are told that the black bear is innocent, but I should not like to trust myself with him." Gibbon muttered in a low tone, "I should not like to trust myself with *you*"—a prudent resolution, says honest Boswell who hated Gibbon, if it referred to a competition of abilities.

The talk went on to patriotism, and Johnson laid down an apophthegm, at "which many will start," many people, in fact, having little sense of humour. Such persons may be reminded for their comfort that at this period patriot had a technical meaning. "Patriotism is the last refuge of a scoundrel." On the 10th of April, he laid down another dogma, calculated to offend the weaker brethren. He defended Pope's line—

Man never *is* but always *to be* blest.

And being asked if man did not sometimes enjoy a momentary happiness, replied, "Never, but when he is drunk." It would be useless to defend these and other such utterances to any one who cannot enjoy them without defence.

On April 11th, the pair went in Reynolds's coach to dine with Cambridge, at Twickenham. Johnson was in high spirits. He remarked as they drove down, upon the

rarity of good humour in life. One friend mentioned by
Boswell was, he said, *acid*, and another *muddy*. At last,
stretching himself and turning with complacency, he
observed, " I look upon myself as a good-humoured fellow "—a bit of self-esteem against which Boswell protested. Johnson, he admitted, was good-natured ; but was
too irascible and impatient to be good-humoured. On
reaching Cambridge's house, Johnson ran to look at the
books. " Mr. Johnson," said Cambridge politely, " I
am going with your pardon to accuse myself, for I have
the same custom which I perceive you have. But it
seems odd that one should have such a desire to look at
the backs of books." " Sir," replied Johnson, wheeling
about at the words, "the reason is very plain. Knowledge is of two kinds. We know a subject ourselves, or
we know where we can find information upon it. When
we inquire into any subject, the first thing we have to do
is to know what books have treated of it. This leads us
to look at catalogues, and the backs of books in libraries."

A pleasant talk followed. Johnson denied the value
attributed to historical reading, on the ground that we
know very little except a few facts and dates. All the
colouring, he said, was conjectural. Boswell chuckles
over the reflection that Gibbon, who was present, did not
take up the cudgels for his favourite study, though the first-
fruits of his labours were to appear in the following year.
"Probably he did not like to trust himself with Johnson."

The conversation presently turned upon the *Beggar's
Opera*, and Johnson sensibly refused to believe that any
man had been made a rogue by seeing it. Yet the moralist
felt bound to utter some condemnation of such a performance, and at last, amidst the smothered amusement of
the company, collected himself to give a heavy stroke :

"there is in it," he said, "such a *labefactation* of all principles as may be dangerous to morality."

A discussion followed as to whether Sheridan was right for refusing to allow his wife to continue as a public singer. Johnson defended him " with all the high spirit of a Roman senator." " He resolved wisely and nobly, to be sure. He is a brave man. Would not a gentleman be disgraced by having his wife sing publicly for hire ? No, sir, there can be no doubt here. I know not if I should not prepare myself for a public singer as readily as let my wife be one."

The stout old supporter of social authority went on to denounce the politics of the day. He asserted that politics had come to mean nothing but the art of rising in the world. He contrasted the absence of any principles with the state of the national mind during the stormy days of the seventeenth century. This gives the pith of Johnston's political prejudices. He hated Whigs blindly from his cradle ; but he justified his hatred on the ground that they were now all " bottomless Whigs," that is to say, that pierce where you would, you came upon no definite creed, but only upon hollow formulæ, intended as a cloak for private interest. If Burke and one or two of his friends be excepted, the remark had but too much justice.

In 1776, Boswell found Johnson rejoicing in the prospect of a journey to Italy with the Thrales. Before starting he was to take a trip to the country, in which Boswell agreed to join. Boswell gathered up various bits of advice before their departure. One seems to have commended itself to him as specially available for practice. " A man who had been drinking freely," said the moralist, " should never go into a new company. He

would probably strike them as ridiculous, though he
might be in unison with those who had been drinking
with him." Johnson propounded another favourite theory.
"A ship," he said, "was worse than a gaol. There is in
a gaol better air, better company, better conveniency of
every kind; and a ship has the additional disadvantage
of being in danger."

On March 19th, they went by coach to the Angel at
Oxford; and next morning visited the Master of University College, who chose with Boswell to act in opposition to a very sound bit of advice given by Johnson
soon afterwards—perhaps with some reference to the proceeding. "Never speak of a man in his own presence; it
is always indelicate and may be offensive." The two, however, discussed Johnson without reserve. The Master said
that he would have given Johnson a hundred pounds for a
discourse on the British Constitution; and Boswell suggested that Johnson should write two volumes of no
great bulk upon Church and State, which should comprise
the whole substance of the argument. "He should erect
a fort on the confines of each." Johnson was not unnaturally displeased with the dialogue, and growled out,
"Why should I be always writing?"

Presently, they went to see Dr. Adams, the doctor's
old friend, who had been answering Hume. Boswell, who
had done his best to court the acquaintance of Voltaire,
Rousseau, Wilkes, and Hume himself, felt it desirable to
reprove Adams for having met Hume with civility. He
aired his admirable sentiments in a long speech, observing
upon the connexion between theory and practice, and remarking, by way of practical application, that, if an infidel
were at once vain and ugly, he might be compared to
"Cicero's beautiful image of Virtue"—which would, as he

seems to think, be a crushing retort. Boswell always
delighted in fighting with his gigantic backer close behind
him. Johnson, as he had doubtless expected, chimed in
with the argument. "You should do your best," said
Johnson, "to diminish the authority, as well as dispute the
arguments of your adversary, because most people are
biased more by personal respect than by reasoning." "You
would not jostle a chimney-sweeper," said Adams. "Yes,"
replied Johnson, "if it were necessary to jostle him
down."

The pair proceeded by post-chaise past Blenheim, and
dined at a good inn at Chapelhouse. Johnston boasted
of the superiority, long since vanished if it ever existed,
of English to French inns, and quoted with great emotion Shenstone's lines—

> Whoe'er has travell'd life's dull round,
> Where'er his stages may have been,
> Must sigh to think he still has found
> The warmest welcome at an inn.

As they drove along rapidly in the post-chaise, he exclaimed, "Life has not many better things than this."
On another occasion he said that he should like to spend
his life driving briskly in a post-chaise with a pretty
woman, clever enough to add to the conversation. The
pleasure was partly owing to the fact that his deafness was
less troublesome in a carriage. But he admitted that
there were drawbacks even to this pleasure. Boswell
asked him whether he would not add a post-chaise journey
to the other sole cause of happiness—namely, drunkenness. "No, sir," said Johnson, "you are driving rapidly
from something or *to* something."

They went to Birmingham, where Boswell pumped

Hector about Johnson's early days, and saw the works of Boulton, Watt's partner, who said to him, "I sell here, sir, what all the world desires to have—*power*." Thence they went to Lichfield, and met more of the rapidly thinning circle of Johnson's oldest friends. Here Boswell was a little scandalized by Johnson's warm exclamation on opening a letter—"One of the most dreadful things that has happened in my time!" This turned out to be the death of Thrale's only son. Boswell thought the phrase too big for the event, and was some time before he could feel a proper concern. He was, however, "curious to observe how Dr. Johnson would be affected," and was again a little scandalized by the reply to his consolatory remark that the Thrales still had daughters. "Sir," said Johnson, "don't you know how you yourself think? Sir, he wishes to propagate his name." The great man was actually putting the family sentiment of a brewer in the same category with the sentiments of the heir of Auchinleck. Johnson, however, calmed down, but resolved to hurry back to London. They stayed a night at Taylor's, who remarked that he had fought a good many battles for a physician, one of their common friends. "But you should consider, sir," said Johnson, "that by every one of your victories he is a loser; for every man of whom you get the better will be very angry, and resolve not to employ him, whereas if people get the better of you in argument about him, they will think 'We'll send for Dr. —— nevertheless!'"

It was after their return to London that Boswell won the greatest triumph of his friendship. He carried through a negotiation, to which, as Burke pleasantly said, there was nothing equal in the whole history of the *corps diplomatique*. At some moment of enthusiasm it had occurred to him to bring Johnson into company with Wilkes. The infidel demagogue was probably in the mind of the Tory High Churchman, when he threw out that pleasant little apophthegm about patriotism. To bring together two such opposites without provoking a collision would be the crowning triumph of Boswell's curiosity. He was ready to run all hazards as a chemist might try some new experiment at the risk of a destructive explosion; but being resolved, he took every precaution with admirable foresight.

Boswell had been invited by the Dillys, well-known booksellers of the day, to meet Wilkes. "Let us have Johnson," suggested the gallant Boswell. "Not for the world!" exclaimed Dilly. But, on Boswell's undertaking the negotiation, he consented to the experiment. Boswell went off to Johnson and politely invited him in Dilly's name. "I will wait upon him," said Johnson. "Provided, sir, I suppose," said the diplomatic Boswell, "that the company which he is to have is agreeable to you." "What do you mean, sir?" exclaimed Johnson. "What do you take me for? Do you think I am so ignorant of the world as to prescribe to a gentleman what company he is to have at his table?" Boswell worked the point a little farther, till, by judicious manipulation, he had got Johnson to commit himself to meeting anybody—even Jack Wilkes, to make a wild hypothesis—at the Dillys' table. Boswell retired, venturing to hope that he had fixed the discussion in Johnson's mind.

The great day arrived, and Boswell, like a consummate general who leaves nothing to chance, went himself to fetch Johnson to the dinner. The great man had forgotten the engagement, and was " buffeting his books " in a dirty shirt and amidst clouds of dust. When reminded

of his promise, he said that he had ordered dinner at
home with Mrs. Williams. Entreaties of the warmest
kind from Boswell softened the peevish old lady, to
whose pleasure Johnson had referred him. Boswell flew
back, announced Mrs. Williams's consent, and Johnson
roared, " Frank, a clean shirt !" and was soon in a hackney-
coach. Boswell rejoiced like a " fortune-hunter who has
got an heiress into a post-chaise with him to set out for
Gretna Green." Yet the joy was with trembling. Arrived
at Dillys', Johnson found himself amongst strangers, and
Boswell watched anxiously from a corner. " Who is that
gentleman ?" whispered Johnson to Dilly. " Mr. Arthur
Lee." Johnson whistled " too-too-too " doubtfully, for
Lee was a patriot and an American. " And who is the
gentleman in lace ?" " Mr. Wilkes, sir." Johnson subsided into a window-seat and fixed his eye on a book.
He was fairly in the toils. His reproof of Boswell was
recent enough to prevent him from exhibiting his dis-
pleasure, and he resolved to restrain himself.

At dinner Wilkes, placed next to Johnson, took up his
part in the performance. He pacified the sturdy moralist
by delicate attentions to his needs. He helped him carefully to some fine veal. " Pray give me leave, sir ; it is
better here—a little of the brown—some fat, sir—a little
of the stuffing—some gravy—let me have the pleasure of
giving you some butter. Allow me to recommend a
squeeze of this orange ; or the lemon, perhaps, may have
more zest." " Sir, sir," cried Johnson, " I am obliged to
you, sir," bowing and turning to him, with a look for
some time of " surly virtue," and soon of complacency.

Gradually the conversation became cordial. Johnson
told of the fascination exercised by Foote, who, like
Wilkes, had succeeded in pleasing him against his will.

Foote once took to selling beer, and it was so bad that the servants of Fitzherbert, one of his customers, resolved to protest. They chose a little black boy to carry their remonstrance; but the boy waited at table one day when Foote was present, and returning to his companions, said, "This is the finest man I have ever seen. I will not deliver your message; I will drink his beer." From Foote the transition was easy to Garrick, whom Johnson, as usual, defended against the attacks of others. He maintained that Garrick's reputation for avarice, though unfounded, had been rather useful than otherwise. "You despise a man for avarice, but you do not hate him." The clamour would have been more effectual, had it been directed against his living with splendour too great for a player. Johnson went on to speak of the difficulty of getting biographical information. When he had wished to write a life of Dryden, he applied to two living men who remembered him. One could only tell him that Dryden had a chair by the fire at Will's Coffee-house in winter, which was moved to the balcony in summer. The other (Cibber) could only report that he remembered Dryden as a "decent old man, arbiter of critical disputes at Will's."

Johnson and Wilkes had one point in common—a vigorous prejudice against the Scotch, and upon this topic they cracked their jokes in friendly emulation. When they met upon a later occasion (1781), they still pursued this inexhaustible subject. Wilkes told how a privateer had completely plundered seven Scotch islands, and re-embarked with three and sixpence. Johnson now remarked in answer to somebody who said "Poor old England is lost!" "Sir, it is not so much to be lamented that old England is lost, as that the Scotch have found it."

K

"You must know, sir," he said to Wilkes, "that I lately took my friend Boswell and showed him genuine civilized life in an English provincial town. I turned him loose at Lichfield, that he might see for once real civility, for you know he lives among savages in Scotland and among rakes in London." "Except," said Wilkes, "when he is with grave, sober, decent people like you and me." "And we ashamed of him," added Johnson, smiling.

Boswell had to bear some jokes against himself and his countrymen from the pair; but he had triumphed, and rejoiced greatly when he went home with Johnson, and heard the great man speak of his pleasant dinner to Mrs. Williams. Johnson seems to have been permanently reconciled to his foe. "Did we not hear so much said of Jack Wilkes," he remarked next year, "we should think more highly of his conversation. Jack has a great variety of talk, Jack is a scholar, and Jack has the manners of a gentleman. But, after hearing his name sounded from pole to pole as the phœnix of convivial felicity, we are disappointed in his company. He has always been at *me*, but I would do Jack a kindness rather than not. The contest is now over."

In fact, Wilkes had ceased to play any part in public life. When Johnson met him next (in 1781) they joked about such dangerous topics as some of Wilkes's political performances. Johnson sent him a copy of the *Lives*, and they were seen conversing *tête-à-tête* in confidential whispers about George II. and the King of Prussia. To Boswell's mind it suggested the happy days when the lion should lie down with the kid, or, as Dr. Barnard suggested, the goat.

In the year 1777 Johnson began the *Lives of the Poets*, in compliance with a request from the booksellers, who wished for prefaces to a large collection of English poetry. Johnson asked for this work the extremely modest sum of 200 guineas, when he might easily, according to Malone, have received 1000 or 1500. He did not meet Boswell till September, when they spent ten days together at Dr. Taylor's. The subject which specially interested Boswell at this time was the fate of the unlucky Dr. Dodd, hanged for forgery in the previous June. Dodd seems to have been a worthless charlatan of the popular preacher variety. His crime would not in our days have been thought worthy of so severe a punishment; but his contemporaries were less shocked by the fact of death being inflicted for such a fault, than by the fact of its being inflicted on a clergyman. Johnson exerted himself to procure a remission of the sentence by writing various letters and petitions on Dodd's behalf. He seems to have been deeply moved by the man's appeal, and could "not bear the thought" that any negligence of his should lead to the death of a fellow-creature ; but he said that if he had himself been in authority he would have signed the death-warrant, and for the man himself he had as little respect as might be. He said, indeed, that Dodd was right in not joining in the "cant" about leaving a wretched world. "No, no," said the poor rogue, "it has been a very agreeable world to me." Dodd had allowed to pass for his own one of the papers composed for him by Johnson, and the Doctor was not quite pleased. When, however, Seward expressed a doubt as to Dodd's power of writing so forcibly, Johnson felt bound not to expose him. "Why should you think so ? Depend upon it, sir, when any man knows he is to be hanged in a fortnight, it concentrates his mind wonderfully." On another occasion, Johnson expressed a doubt himself as to whether Dodd had really composed a certain prayer on the night before his execution. "Sir, do you think that a man the night before he is to be hanged cares for the succession of the royal family? Though he *may* have composed this prayer then. A man who has been canting all his life may cant to the last; and yet a man who has been refused a pardon after so much petitioning, would hardly be praying thus fervently for the king."

The last day at Taylor's was characteristic. Johnson was very cordial to his disciple, and Boswell fancied that he could defend his master at "the point of his sword." "My regard for you," said Johnson, "is greater almost than I have words to express, but I do not choose to be always repeating it. Write it down in the first leaf of your pocket-book, and never doubt of it again." They became sentimental, and talked of the misery of human life. Boswell spoke of the pleasures of society. "Alas, sir," replied Johnson, like a true pessimist, "these are only struggles for happiness!" He felt exhilarated, he said, when he first went to Ranelagh, but he changed to the mood of Xerxes weeping at the sight of his army. "It went to my heart to consider that there was not one in all that brilliant circle that was not afraid to go home and think; but that the thoughts of each individual would be distressing when alone." Some years before he had gone with Boswell to the Pantheon and taken a more cheerful view. When Boswell doubted whether there were many happy people present, he said, "Yes, sir, there are many happy people here. There are many people here who are watching hundreds, and who think hundreds are watching them." The more permanent feeling was that which he expressed in the "serene autumn night" in Taylor's garden. He was willing, however, to talk

calmly about eternal punishment, and to admit the possibility of a "mitigated interpretation."

After supper he dictated to Boswell an argument in
favour of the negro who was then claiming his liberty in
Scotland. He hated slavery with a zeal which the excellent Boswell thought to be "without knowledge;" and on
one occasion gave as a toast to some "very grave men"
at Oxford, "Here's to the next insurrection of negroes in
the West Indies." The hatred was combined with as
hearty a dislike for American independence. "How is
it," he said, "that we always hear the loudest yelps for
liberty amongst the drivers of negroes?" The harmony
of the evening was unluckily spoilt by an explosion of
this prejudice. Boswell undertook the defence of the
colonists, and the discussion became so fierce that though
Johnson had expressed a willingness to sit up all night
with him, they were glad to part after an hour or two, and
go to bed.

In 1778, Boswell came to London and found Johnson
absorbed, to an extent which apparently excited his jealousy, by his intimacy with the Thrales. They had, however, several agreeable meetings. One was at the club,
and Boswell's report of the conversation is the fullest
that we have of any of its meetings. A certain reserve
is indicated by his using initials for the interlocutors, of
whom, however, one can be easily identified as Burke.
The talk began by a discussion of an antique statue, said
to be the dog of Alcibiades, and valued at 1000*l.* Burke
said that the representation of no animal could be worth
so much. Johnson, whose taste for art was a vanishing
quantity, said that the value was proportional to the difficulty. A statue, as he argued on another occasion, would
be worth nothing if it were cut out of a carrot. Every-

thing, he now said, was valuable which "enlarged the sphere of human powers." The first man who balanced a straw upon his nose, or rode upon three horses at once, deserved the applause of mankind; and so statues of animals should be preserved as a proof of dexterity, though men should not continue such fruitless labours.

The conversation became more instructive under the guidance of Burke. He maintained what seemed to his hearers a paradox, though it would be interesting to hear his arguments from some profounder economist than Boswell, that a country would be made more populous by emigration. "There are bulls enough in Ireland," he remarked incidentally in the course of the argument. "So, sir, I should think from your argument," said Johnson, for once condescending to an irresistible pun. It is recorded, too, that he once made a bull himself, observing that a horse was so slow that when it went up hill, it stood still. If he now failed to appreciate Burke's argument, he made one good remark. Another speaker said that unhealthy countries were the most populous. "Countries which are the most populous," replied Johnson, "have the most destructive diseases. That is the true state of the proposition;" and indeed, the remark applies to the case of emigration.

A discussion then took place as to whether it would be worth while for Burke to take so much trouble with speeches which never decided a vote. Burke replied that a speech, though it did not gain one vote, would have an influence, and maintained that the House of Commons was not wholly corrupt. "We are all more or less governed by interest," was Johnson's comment. "But interest will not do everything. In a case which admits of doubt, we try to think on the side which is for our interest, and generally bring ourselves to act accordingly. But the subject must admit of diversity of colouring; it must receive a colour on that side. In the House of Commons there are members enough who will not vote what is grossly absurd and unjust. No, sir, there must always be right enough, or appearance of right, to keep wrong in countenance." After some deviations, the conversation returned to this point. Johnson and Burke agreed on a characteristic statement. Burke said that from his experience he had learnt to think better of mankind. "From my experience," replied Johnson, "I have found them worse on commercial dealings, more disposed to cheat than I had any notion of; but more disposed to do one another good than I had conceived." "Less just, and more beneficent," as another speaker suggested. Johnson proceeded to say that considering the pressure of want, it was wonderful that men would do so much for each other. The greatest liar is said to speak more truth than falsehood, and perhaps the worst man might do more good than not. But when Boswell suggested that perhaps experience might increase our estimate of human happiness, Johnson returned to his habitual pessimism. "No, sir, the more we inquire, the more we shall find men less happy." The talk soon wandered off into a disquisition upon the folly of deliberately testing the strength of our friend's affection.

The evening ended by Johnson accepting a commission to write to a friend who had given to the Club a hogshead of claret, and to request another, with "a happy ambiguity of expression," in the hopes that it might also be a present.

Some days afterwards, another conversation took place, which has a certain celebrity in Boswellian literature. The scene was at Dilly's, and the guests included Miss

Seward and Mrs. Knowles, a well-known Quaker Lady.
Before dinner Johnson seized upon a book which he kept
in his lap during dinner, wrapped up in the table-cloth.
His attention was not distracted from the serious business
of the hour, but he hit upon a topic which happily combined the two appropriate veins of thought. He boasted
that he would write a cookery-book upon philosophical
principles; and declared in opposition to Miss Seward
that such a task was beyond the sphere of woman. Perhaps this led to a discussion upon the privileges of men, in
which Johnson put down Mrs. Knowles, who had some
hankering for women's rights, by the Shakspearian
maxim that if two men ride on a horse, one must ride
behind. Driven from her position in this world, poor
Mrs. Knowles hoped that sexes might be equal in the
next. Boswell reproved her by the remark already quoted,
that men might as well expect to be equal to angels. He
enforces this view by an illustration suggested by the
"Rev. Mr. Brown of Utrecht," who had observed that a
great or small glass might be equally full, though not
holding equal quantities. Mr. Brown intended this for a
confutation of Hume, who has said that a little Miss,
dressed for a ball, may be as happy as an orator who has
won some triumphant success.[1]

The conversation thus took a theological turn, and
Mrs. Knowles was fortunate enough to win Johnson's
high approval. He defended a doctrine maintained by
Soame Jenyns, that friendship is *not* a Christian virtue.
Mrs. Knowles remarked that Jesus had twelve disciples,

[1] Boswell remarks as a curious coincidence that the same illus-
tration had been used by a Dr. King, a dissenting minister.
Doubtless it has been used often enough. For one instance see
Donne's Sermons (Alford's Edition), vol. i., p. 5.

but there was *one* whom he *loved*. Johnson, "with eyes sparkling benignantly," exclaimed, "Very well indeed, madam ; you have said very well !"

So far all had gone smoothly ; but here, for some inexplicable reason, Johnson burst into a sudden fury against the American rebels, whom he described as " rascals, robbers, pirates," and roared out a tremendous volley, which might almost have been audible across the Atlantic. Boswell sat and trembled, but gradually diverted the sage to less exciting topics. The name of Jonathan Edwards suggested a discussion upon free will and necessity, upon which poor Boswell was much given to worry himself. Some time afterwards Johnson wrote to him, in answer to one of his lamentations : "I hoped you had got rid of all this hypocrisy of misery. What have you to do with liberty and necessity ? Or what more than to hold your tongue about it ?" Boswell could never take this sensible advice ; but he got little comfort from his oracle. "We know that we are all free, and there's an end on't," was his statement on one occasion, and now he could only say, " All theory is against the freedom of the will, and all experience for it."

Some familiar topics followed, which play a great part in Boswell's reports. Among the favourite topics of the sentimentalists of the day was the denunciation of "luxury," and of civilized life in general. There was a disposition to find in the South Sea savages or American Indians an embodiment of the fancied state of nature. Johnson heartily despised the affectation. He was told of an American woman who had to be bound in order to keep her from savage life. " She must have been an animal, a beast," said Boswell. " Sir," said Johnson, " she was a speaking cat." Somebody quoted

to him with admiration the soliloquy of an officer who
had lived in the wilds of America : "Here am I, free and
unrestrained, amidst the rude magnificence of nature, with
the Indian woman by my side, and this gun, with which
I can procure food when I want it! What more can
be desired for human happiness?" "Do not allow yourself, sir," replied Johnson, "to be imposed upon by such
gross absurdity. It is sad stuff; it is brutish. If a bull
could speak, he might as well exclaim, 'Here am I with
this cow and this grass; what being can enjoy greater
felicity?'" When Johnson implored Boswell to "clear
his mind of cant," he was attacking his disciple for affecting a serious depression about public affairs; but the cant
which he hated would certainly have included as its first
article an admiration for the state of nature.

On the present occasion Johnson defended luxury, and
said that he had learnt much from Mandeville—a shrewd
cynic, in whom Johnson's hatred for humbug is exaggerated into a general disbelief in real as well as sham
nobleness of sentiment. As the conversation proceeded,
Johnson expressed his habitual horror of death, and
caused Miss Seward's ridicule by talking seriously of
ghosts and the importance of the question of their reality ;
and then followed an explosion, which seems to have
closed this characteristic evening. A young woman had
become a Quaker under the influence of Mrs. Knowles,
who now proceeded to deprecate Johnson's wrath at what
he regarded as an apostasy. "Madam," he said, "she is
an odious wench," and he proceeded to denounce her
audacity in presuming to choose a religion for herself.
"She knew no more of the points of difference," he said,
"than of the difference between the Copernican and
Ptolemaic systems." When Mrs. Knowles said that she

had the New Testament before her, he said that it was the " most difficult book in the world," and he proceeded to attack the unlucky proselyte with a fury which shocked the two ladies. Mrs. Knowles afterwards published a report of this conversation, and obtained another report, with which, however, she was not satisfied, from Miss Seward. Both of them represent the poor doctor as hopelessly confuted by the mild dignity and calm reason of Mrs. Knowles, though the triumph is painted in far the brightest colours by Mrs. Knowles herself. Unluckily, there is not a trace of Johnson's manner, except in one phrase, in either report, and they are chiefly curious as an indirect testimony to Boswell's superior powers. The passage, in which both the ladies agree, is that Johnson, on the expression of Mrs. Knowles's hope that he would meet the young lady in another world, retorted that he was not fond of meeting fools anywhere.

Poor Boswell was at this time a water-drinker by Johnson's recommendation, though unluckily for himself he never broke off his drinking habits for long. They had a conversation at Paoli's, in which Boswell argued against his present practice. Johnson remarked " that wine gave a man nothing, but only put in motion what had been locked up in frost." It was a key, suggested some one, which opened a box, but the box might be full or empty. " Nay, sir," said Johnson, " conversation is the key, wine is a picklock, which forces open the box and injures it. A man should cultivate his mind, so as to have that confidence and readiness without wine which wine gives." Boswell characteristically said that the great difficulty was from " benevolence." It was hard to refuse " a good, worthy man " who asked you to try his cellar. This, according to Johnson, was mere conceit, implying an exaggerated estimate of your importance to your entertainer. Reynolds gallantly took up the opposite side, and produced the one recorded instance of a Johnsonian blush. " I won't argue any more with you, sir," said Johnson, who thought every man to be elevated who drank wine, " you are too far gone." " I should have thought so indeed, sir, had I made such a speech as you have now done," said Reynolds ; and Johnson apologized with the aforesaid blush.

The explosion was soon over on this occasion. Not long afterwards, Johnson attacked Boswell so fiercely at a dinner at Reynolds's, that the poor disciple kept away for a week. They made it up when they met next, and Johnson solaced Boswell's wounded vanity by highly commending an image made by him to express his feelings. " I don't care how often or how high Johnson tosses me, when only friends are present, for then I fall upon soft ground ; but I do not like falling on stones, which is the case when enemies are present." The phrase may recall one of Johnson's happiest illustrations. When some one said in his presence that a congé d'élire might be considered as only a strong recommendation : " Sir," replied Johnson, " it is such a recommendation as if I should throw you out of a two-pair of stairs window, and recommend you to fall soft."

It is perhaps time to cease these extracts from Boswell's reports. The next two years were less fruitful, In 1779 Boswell was careless, though twice in London, and in 1780, he did not pay his annual visit. Boswell has partly filled up the gap by a collection of sayings made by Langton, some passages from which have been quoted, and his correspondence gives various details. Garrick died in January of 1779, and Beauclerk in

March, 1780. Johnson himself seems to have shown few symptoms of increasing age; but a change was approaching, and the last years of his life were destined to be clouded, not merely by physical weakness, but by a change of circumstances which had great influence upon his happiness.

CHAPTER V

THE CLOSING YEARS OF JOHNSON'S LIFE.

IN following Boswell's guidance we have necessarily seen only one side of Johnson's life; and probably that side which had least significance for the man himself.

Boswell saw in him chiefly the great dictator of conversation; and though the reports of Johnson's talk represent his character in spite of some qualifications with unusual fulness, there were many traits very inadequately revealed at the Mitre or the Club, at Mrs. Thrale's, or in meetings with Wilkes or Reynolds. We may catch some glimpses from his letters and diaries of that inward life which consisted generally in a long succession of struggles against an oppressive and often paralysing melancholy. Another most noteworthy side to his character is revealed in his relations to persons too humble for admission to the tables at which he exerted a despotic sway. Upon this side Johnson was almost entirely loveable. We often have to regret the imperfection of the records of

> That best portion of a good man's life,
> His little, nameless, unremembered acts
> Of kindness and of love.

Everywhere in Johnson's letters and in the occasional anecdotes, we come upon indications of a tenderness and untiring benevolence which would make us forgive

far worse faults than have ever been laid to his charge.
Nay, the very asperity of the man's outside becomes en-
deared to us by the association.   His irritability never
vented itself against the helpless, and his rough impatience of fanciful troubles implied no want of sympathy
for real sorrow.   One of Mrs. Thrale's anecdotes is intended to show Johnson's harshness :—" When I one day
lamented the loss of a first cousin killed in America,
' Pr'ythee, my dear,' said he, ' have done with canting;
how would the world be the worse for it, I may ask, if all
your relations were at once spitted like larks and roasted
for Presto's supper ? '   Presto was the dog that lay under
the table while we talked."   The counter version, given
by Boswell is, that Mrs. Thrale related her cousin's death
in the midst of a hearty supper, and that Johnson, shocked
at her want of feeling, said, " Madam, it would give *you*
very little concern if all your relations were spitted like
those larks, and roasted for Presto's supper."   Taking the
most unfavourable version, we may judge how much real
indifference to human sorrow was implied by seeing how
Johnson was affected by a loss of one of his humblest
friends.   It is but one case of many.   In 1767, he took
leave, as he notes in his diary, of his " dear old friend,
Catherine Chambers," who had been for about forty-three
years in the service of his family.   " I desired all to with-
draw," he says, " then told her that we were to part for
ever, and, as Christians, we should part with prayer, and
that I would, if she was willing, say a short prayer beside
her. She expressed great desire to hear me, and held up her
poor hands as she lay in bed, with great fervour, while I
prayed, kneeling by her, in nearly the following words "—
which shall not be repeated here—" I then kissed her,"
he adds.   " She told me that to part was the greatest pain

that she had ever felt, and that she hoped we should meet
again in a better place. I expressed, with swelled eyes,
and great emotion of kindness, the same hopes. We
kissed and parted—I humbly hope to meet again and part
no more."

A man with so true and tender a heart could say
sincerely, what with some men would be a mere excuse for
want of sympathy, that he "hated to hear people whine
about metaphysical distresses when there was so much want
and hunger in the world." He had a sound and righteous
contempt for all affectation of excessive sensibility. Suppose, said Boswell to him, whilst their common friend
Baretti was lying under a charge of murder, "that one of
your intimate friends were apprehended for an offence for
which he might be hanged." "I should do what I could,"
replied Johnson, "to bail him, and give him any other
assistance ; but if he were once fairly hanged, I should
not suffer." "Would you eat your dinner that day, sir ? "
asks Boswell.   "Yes, sir ; and eat it as if he were eating
with me. Why there's Baretti, who's to be tried for his
life to-morrow. Friends have risen up for him upon every
side ; yet if he should be hanged, none of them will eat a
slice of plum-pudding the less. Sir, that sympathetic
feeling goes a very little way in depressing the mind."
Boswell illustrated the subject by saying that Tom Davies
had just written a letter to Foote, telling him that he could
not sleep from concern about Baretti, and at the same
time recommending a young man who kept a pickle-shop.
Johnson summed up by the remark : "You will find
these very feeling people are not very ready to do you
good. They *pay* you by *feeling*." Johnson never objected
to feeling, but to the waste of feeling.

In a similar vein he told Mrs. Thrale that a " surly fellow " like himself had no compassion to spare for "wounds given to vanity and softness," whilst witnessing the common sight of actual want in great cities. On Lady Tavistock's death, said to have been caused by grief for her husband's loss, he observed that her life might have been saved if she had been put into a small chandler's shop, with a child to nurse. When Mrs. Thrale suggested that a lady would be grieved because her friend had lost the chance of a fortune, " She will suffer as much, perhaps," he replied, "as your horse did when your cow miscarried." Mrs. Thrale testifies that he once reproached her sternly for complaining of the dust. When he knew, he said, how many poor families would perish next winter for want of the bread which the drought would deny, he could not bear to hear ladies sighing for rain on account of their complexions or their clothes. While reporting such sayings, she adds, that he loved the poor as she never saw any one else love them, with an earnest desire to make them happy. His charity was unbounded ; he proposed to allow himself one hundred a year out of the three hundred of his pension ; but the Thrales could never discover that he really spent upon himself more than 70*l.*, or at most 80*l.* He had numerous dependants, abroad as well as at home, who "did not like to see him latterly, unless he brought 'em money." He filled his pockets with small cash which he distributed to beggars in defiance of political economy. When told that the recipients only laid it out upon gin or tobacco, he replied that it was savage to deny them the few coarse pleasures which the richer disdained. Numerous instances are given of more judicious charity. When, for example, a Benedictine monk, whom he had seen in Paris, became a Protestant, Johnson supported him for some months in London, till he could get a living.

L

Once coming home late at night, he found a poor woman
lying in the street. He carried her to his house on his
back, and found that she was reduced to the lowest stage
of want, poverty, and disease. He took care of her at his
own charge, with all tenderness, until she was restored
to health, and tried to have her put into a virtuous way of
living. His house, in his later years, was filled with
various waifs and strays, to whom he gave hospitality and
sometimes support, defending himself by saying that if he
did not help them nobody else would. The head of his
household was Miss Williams, who had been a friend of
his wife's, and after coming to stay with him, in order to
undergo an operation for cataract, became a permanent
inmate of his house. She had a small income of some
40l. a year, partly from the charity of connexions of her
father's, and partly arising from a little book of miscel-
lanies published by subscription. She was a woman of
some sense and cultivation, and when she died (in 1783)
Johnson said that for thirty years she had been to him as
a sister. Boswell's jealousy was excited during the first
period of his acquaintance, when Goldsmith one night
went home with Johnson, crying " I go to Miss Williams "
—a phrase which implied admission to an intimacy from
which Boswell was as yet excluded. Boswell soon obtained
the coveted privilege, and testifies to the respect with
which Johnson always treated the inmates of his family.
Before leaving her to dine with Boswell at the hotel, he
asked her what little delicacy should be sent to her from
the tavern. Poor Miss Williams, however, was peevish,
and, according to Hawkins, had been known to drive Johnson out of the room by her reproaches, and Boswell's
delicacy was shocked by the supposition that she tested the
fulness of cups of tea, by putting her finger inside. We are

glad to know that this was a false impression, and, in fact, Miss Williams, however unfortunate in temper and circumstances, seems to have been a lady by manners and education.

The next inmate of this queer household was Robert Levett, a man who had been a waiter at a coffee-house in Paris frequented by surgeons. They had enabled him to pick up some of their art, and he set up as an " obscure practiser in physic amongst the lower people" in London. He took from them such fees as he could get, including provisions, sometimes, unfortunately for him, of the potable kind. He was once entrapped into a queer marriage, and Johnson had to arrange a separation from his wife. Johnson, it seems, had a good opinion of his medical skill, and more or less employed his services in that capacity. He attended his patron at his breakfast ; breakfasting, said Percy, "on the crust of a roll, which Johnson threw to him after tearing out the crumb." The phrase, it is said, goes too far ; Johnson always took pains that Levett should be treated rather as a friend than as a dependant.

Besides these humble friends, there was a Mrs. Desmoulins, the daughter of a Lichfield physician. Johnson had had some quarrel with the father in his youth for revealing a confession of the mental disease which tortured him from early years. He supported Mrs. Desmoulins none the less, giving house-room to her and her daughter, and making her an allowance of half-a-guinea a week, a sum equal to a twelfth part of his pension. Francis Barber has already been mentioned, and we have a dim vision of a Miss Carmichael, who completed what he facetiously called his " seraglio." It was anything but a happy family. He summed up their relations in a letter

to Mrs. Thrale. "Williams," he says, "hates everybody;
Levett hates Desmoulins, and does not love Williams;
Desmoulins hates them both; Poll (Miss Carmichael)
loves none of them." Frank Barber complained of Miss
Williams's authority, and Miss Williams of Frank's in-
subordination. Intruders who had taken refuge under
his roof, brought their children there in his absence, and
grumbled if their dinners were ill-dressed. The old man
bore it all, relieving himself by an occasional growl, but
reproaching any who ventured to join in the growl for
their indifference to the sufferings of poverty. Levett
died in January, 1782; Miss Williams died, after a linger-
ing illness, in 1783, and Johnson grieved in solitude for
the loss of his testy companions. A poem, composed
upon Levett's death, records his feelings in language which
wants the refinement of Goldsmith or the intensity of
Cowper's pathos, but which is yet so sincere and tender
as to be more impressive than far more elegant compositions. It will be a fitting close to this brief indication
of one side of Johnson's character, too easily overlooked
in Boswell's pages, to quote part of what Thackeray truly
calls the " sacred verses " upon Levett :—

> Well tried through many a varying year
>   See Levett to the grave descend,
> Officious, innocent, sincere,
>   Of every friendless name the friend.
>
> In misery's darkest cavern known,
>   His ready help was ever nigh;
> Where hopeless anguish pour'd his groan,
>   And lonely want retired to die.
>
> No summons mock'd by dull delay,
>   No petty gains disdain'd by pride;
> The modest wants of every day,
>   The toil of every day supplied.

> His virtues walk'd their narrow round,
>   Nor made a pause, nor left a void ;
> And sure the eternal Master found
>   His single talent well employ'd.
>
> The busy day, the peaceful night,
>   Unfelt, uncounted, glided by ;
> His frame was firm, his eye was bright,
>   Though now his eightieth year was nigh.
>
> Then, with no throbs of fiery pain,
>   No cold gradations of decay,
> Death broke at once the vital chain,
>   And freed his soul the easiest way.

The last stanza smells somewhat of the country tomb-
stone ; but to read the whole and to realize the deep,
manly sentiment which it implies, without tears in one's
eyes is to me at least impossible.

There is one little touch which may be added before we
proceed to the closing years of this tender-hearted old
moralist. Johnson loved little children, calling them
" little dears," and cramming them with sweetmeats,
though we regret to add that he once snubbed a little
child rather severely for a want of acquaintance with the
Pilgrim's Progress. His cat, Hodge, should be famous
amongst the lovers of the race. He used to go out and
buy oysters for Hodge, that the servants might not take
a dislike to the animal from having to serve it themselves.
He reproached his wife for beating a cat before the maid,
lest she should give a precedent for cruelty. Boswell,
who cherished an antipathy to cats, suffered at seeing
Hodge scrambling up Johnson's breast, whilst he
smiled and rubbed the beast's back and pulled its tail.
Bozzy remarked that he was a fine cat. " Why, yes, sir,"
said Johnson ; " but I have had cats whom I liked better

than this," and then, lest Hodge should be put out of countenance, he added, "but he is a very fine cat, a very fine cat indeed." He told Langton once of a young gentleman who, when last heard of, was "running about town shooting cats; but," he murmured in a kindly reverie, "Hodge shan't be shot; no, no, Hodge shall not be shot!" Once, when Johnson was staying at a house in Wales, the gardener brought in a hare which had been caught in the potatoes. The order was given to take it to the cook. Johnson asked to have it placed in his arms. He took it to the window and let it go, shouting to increase its speed. When his host complained that he had perhaps spoilt the dinner, Johnson replied by insisting that the rights of hospitality included an animal which had thus placed itself under the protection of the master of the garden.

We must proceed, however, to a more serious event. The year 1781 brought with it a catastrophe which profoundly affected the brief remainder of Johnson's life. Mr. Thrale, whose health had been shaken by fits, died suddenly on the 4th of April. The ultimate consequence was Johnson's loss of the second home, in which he had so often found refuge from melancholy, alleviation of physical suffering, and pleasure in social converse. The change did not follow at once, but as the catastrophe of a little social drama, upon the rights and wrongs of which a good deal of controversy has been expended.

Johnson was deeply affected by the loss of a friend whose face, as he said, "had never been turned upon him through fifteen years but with respect and benignity." He wrote solemn and affecting letters to the widow, and busied himself strenuously in her service. Thrale had made him one of his executors, leaving him a small

legacy; and Johnson took, it seems, a rather simple-
minded pleasure in dealing with important commercial
affairs and signing cheques for large sums of money. The
old man of letters, to whom three hundred a year had
been superabundant wealth, was amused at finding himself
in the position of a man of business, regulating what was
then regarded as a princely fortune. The brewery was
sold after a time, and Johnson bustled about with an ink-
horn and pen in his button-hole. When asked what was
the value of the property, he replied magniloquently,
" We are not here to sell a parcel of boilers and vats, but
the potentiality of growing rich beyond the dreams of
avarice." The brewery was in fact sold to Barclay,
Perkins, and Co. for the sum of 135,000l., and some
years afterwards it was the largest concern of the kind in
the world.

The first effect of the change was probably rather to
tighten than to relax the bond of union with the Thrale
family. During the winter of 1781-2, Johnson's infirmities were growing upon him. In the beginning of
1782 he was suffering from an illness which excited
serious apprehensions, and he went to Mrs. Thrale's, as the
only house where he could use " all the freedom that
sickness requires." She nursed him carefully, and expressed her feelings with characteristic vehemence in a
curious journal which he had encouraged her to keep. It
records her opinions about her affairs and her family, with
a frankness remarkable even in writing intended for no
eye but her own. " Here is Mr. Johnson very ill," she
writes on the 1st of February ; . . . . " What shall we do
for him ? If I lose *him*, I am more than undone—friend,
father, guardian, confidant ! God give me health and
patience ! What shall I do ?" There is no reason to

doubt the sincerity of these sentiments, though they seem
to represent a mood of excitement. They show that for
ten months after Thrale's death Mrs. Thrale was keenly
sensitive to the value of Johnson's friendship.

A change, however, was approaching. Towards the
end of 1780 Mrs. Thrale had made the acquaintance of an
Italian musician named Piozzi, a man of amiable and
honourable character, making an independent income by
his profession, but to the eyes of most people rather inoffensive than specially attractive. The friendship between
Mrs. Thrale and Piozzi rapidly became closer, and by the
end of 1781 she was on very intimate terms with the
gentleman whom she calls " my Piozzi." He had been
making a professional trip to the Continent during part
of the period since her husband's death, and upon his
return in November, Johnson congratulated her upon having
two friends who loved her, in terms which suggest no
existing feeling of jealousy. During 1782 the mutual
affection of the lady and the musician became stronger,
and in the autumn they had avowed it to each other, and
were discussing the question of marriage.

No one who has had some experience of life will be
inclined to condemn Mrs. Thrale for her passion. Rather
the capacity for a passion not excited by an intrinsically
unworthy object should increase our esteem for her. Her
marriage with Thrale had been, as has been said, one of
convenience ; and, though she bore him many children
and did her duty faithfully, she never loved him. Towards the end of his life he had made her jealous by very
marked attentions to the pretty and sentimental Sophy
Streatfield, which once caused a scene at his table ; and
during the last two years his mind had been weakened,
and his conduct had caused her anxiety and discomfort.

It is not surprising that she should welcome the warm
and simple devotion of her new lover, though she was of
a ripe age and the mother of grown-up daughters.
It is, however, equally plain that an alliance with a
foreign fiddler was certain to shock British respectability.
It is the old story of the quarrel between Philistia and
Bohemia. Nor was respectability without much to say
for itself. Piozzi was a Catholic as well as a foreigner;
to marry him was in all probability to break with daughters just growing into womanhood, whom it was obviously
her first duty to protect. The marriage, therefore, might
be regarded as not merely a revolt against conventional
morality, but as leading to a desertion of country, religion,
and family. Her children, her husband's friends, and her
whole circle were certain to look upon the match with
feelings of the strongest disapproval, and she admitted to
herself that the objections were founded upon something
more weighty than a fear of the world's censure.

Johnson, in particular, among whose virtues one
cannot reckon a superiority to British prejudice, would
inevitably consider the marriage as simply degrading.
Foreseeing this, and wishing to avoid the pain of rejecting
advice which she felt unable to accept, she refrained
from retaining her "friend, father, and guardian" in the
position of "confidant." Her situation in the summer of
1782 was therefore exceedingly trying. She was unhappy
at home. Her children, she complains, did not love her;
her servants "devoured" her; her friends censured her;
and her expenses were excessive, whilst the loss of a
lawsuit strained her resources. Johnson, sickly, suffering
and descending into the gloom of approaching decay,
was present like a charged thunder-cloud ready to burst
at any moment, if she allowed him to approach the chief

subject of her thoughts. Though not in love with Mrs.
Thrale, he had a very intelligible feeling of jealousy
towards any one who threatened to distract her allegiance.
Under such circumstances we might expect the state of
things which Miss Burney described long afterwards
(though with some confusion of dates). Mrs. Thrale,
she says, was absent and agitated, restless in manner,
and hurried in speech, forcing smiles, and averting her
eyes from her friends ; neglecting every one, including
Johnson and excepting only Miss Burney herself, to
whom the secret was confided, and the situation therefore
explained. Gradually, according to Miss Burney, she
became more petulant to Johnson than she was herself
aware, gave palpable hints of being worried by his company, and finally excited his resentment and suspicion.
In one or two utterances, though he doubtless felt the
expedience of reserve, he intrusted his forebodings to
Miss Burney, and declared that Streatham was lost to
him for ever.

At last, in the end of August, the crisis came. Mrs.
Thrale's lawsuit had gone against her. She thought it
desirable to go abroad and save money. It had moreover been "long her dearest wish" to see Italy, with
Piozzi for a guide. The one difficulty (as she says in her
journal at the time), was that it seemed equally hard to
part with Johnson or to take him with her till he had
regained strength. At last, however she took courage to
confide to him her plans for travel. To her extreme annoyance he fully approved of them. He advised her to
go ; anticipated her return in two or three years ; and told
her daughter that he should not accompany them, even if
invited. No behaviour, it may be admitted, could be
more provoking than this unforeseen reasonableness. To

nerve oneself to part with a friend, and to find the friend perfectly ready, and all your battery of argument thrown away is most vexatious. The poor man should have begged her to stay with him, or to take him with her; he should have made the scene which she professed to dread, but which would have been the best proof of her power. The only conclusion which could really have satisfied her—though she, in all probability, did not know it—would have been an outburst which would have justified a rupture, and allowed her to protest against his tyranny as she now proceeded to protest against his complacency.

Johnson wished to go to Italy two years later; and his present willingness to be left was probably caused by a growing sense of the dangers which threatened their friendship. Mrs. Thrale's anger appears in her journal. He had never really loved her, she declares; his affection for her had been interested, though even in her wrath she admits that he really loved her husband; he cared less for her conversation, which she had fancied necessary to his existence, than for her "roast beef and plumb pudden," which he now devours too "dirtily for endurance." She was fully resolved to go, and yet she could not bear that her going should fail to torture the friend whom for eighteen years she had loved and cherished so kindly.

No one has a right at once to insist upon the compliance of his friends, and to insist that it should be a painful compliance. Still Mrs. Thrale's petulant outburst was natural enough. It requires notice because her subsequent account of the rupture has given rise to attacks on Johnson's character. Her "Anecdotes," written in 1785, show that her real affection for Johnson was still coloured by resentment for his conduct at this and a later period. They have an apologetic character which shows itself in a statement as to the origin of the quarrel, curiously different from the contemporary accounts in the diary. She says substantially, and the whole book is written so as to give probability to the assertion, that Johnson's bearishness and demands upon her indulgence had become intolerable, when he was no longer under restraint from her husband's presence. She therefore " took advantage " of her lost lawsuit and other troubles to leave London, and thus escape from his domestic tyranny. He no longer, as she adds, suffered from anything but " old age and general infirmity " (a tolerably wide exception !), and did not require her nursing. She therefore withdrew from the yoke to which she had contentedly submitted during her husband's life, but which was intolerable when her " coadjutor was no more."

Johnson's society was, we may easily believe, very trying to a widow in such a position ; and it seems to be true that Thrale was better able than Mrs. Thrale to restrain his oddities, little as the lady shrunk at times from reasonable plain-speaking. But the later account involves something more than a bare suppression of the truth. The excuse about his health is, perhaps, the worst part of her case, because obviously insincere. Nobody could be more fully aware than Mrs. Thrale that Johnson's infirmities were rapidly gathering, and that another winter or two must in all probability be fatal to him. She knew, therefore, that he was never more in want of the care which, as she seems to imply, had saved him from the specific tendency to something like madness. She knew, in fact, that she was throwing him upon the care of his other friends, zealous and affectionate enough, it is true, but yet unable to supply him with the domestic comforts of Streatham. She clearly felt that this was a real injury, inevitable it might be under the circumstances, but certainly not to be extenuated by the paltry evasion as to his improved health. So far from Johnson's health being now established, she had not dared to speak until his temporary recovery from a dangerous illness, which had provoked her at the time to the strongest expressions of anxious regret. She had (according to the diary) regarded a possible breaking of the yoke in the early part of 1782 as a terrible evil, which would "more than ruin her." Even when resolved to leave Streatham, her one great difficulty is the dread of parting with Johnson, and the pecuniary troubles are the solid and conclusive reason. In the later account the money question is the mere pretext; the desire to leave Johnson the true motive; and the long-cherished desire to see Italy with Piozzi is judiciously dropped out of notice altogether.

The truth is plain enough. Mrs. Thrale was torn by conflicting feelings. She still loved Johnson, and yet dreaded his certain disapproval of her strongest wishes. She respected him, but was resolved not to follow his advice. She wished to treat him with kindness and to be repaid with gratitude, and yet his presence and his affection were full of intolerable inconveniences. When an old friendship becomes a burden, the smaller infirmities of manner and temper to which we once submitted willingly, become intolerable. She had borne with Johnson's modes of eating and with his rough reproofs to herself and her friends during sixteen years of her married life; and for nearly a year of her widowhood she still clung to him as the wisest and kindest of monitors. His manners had undergone no spasmodic change. They became intolerable

when, for other reasons, she resented his possible interference, and wanted a very different guardian and confidant; and, therefore, she wished to part, and yet wished
that the initiative should come from him.

The decision to leave Streatham was taken. Johnson
parted with deep regret from the house; he read a chapter
of the Testament in the library; he took leave of the
church with a kiss; he composed a prayer commending
the family to the protection of Heaven; and he did not
forget to note in his journal the details of the last dinner
of which he partook. This quaint observation may
have been due to some valetudinary motive, or, more probably, to some odd freak of association. Once, when
eating an omelette, he was deeply affected because it
recalled his old friend Nugent. " Ah, my dear friend,"
he said " in an agony," " I shall never eat omelette with
thee again!" And in the present case there is an obscure
reference to some funeral connected in his mind with a
meal. The unlucky entry has caused some ridicule, but
need hardly convince us that his love of the family in
which for so many years he had been an honoured and
honour-giving inmate was, as Miss Seward amiably sug-
gests, in great measure " kitchen-love."

No immediate rupture followed the abandonment of
the Streatham establishment. Johnson spent some weeks
at Brighton with Mrs. Thrale, during which a crisis was
taking place, without his knowledge, in her relations to
Piozzi. After vehement altercations with her daughters,
whom she criticizes with great bitterness for their utter
want of heart, she resolved to break with Piozzi for at
least a time. Her plan was to go to Bath, and there to
retrench her expenses, in the hopes of being able to recall
her lover at some future period. Meanwhile he left her

and returned to Italy. After another winter in London, during which Johnson was still a frequent inmate of her house, she went to Bath with her daughters in April, 1783. A melancholy period followed for both the friends. Mrs. Thrale lost a younger daughter, and Johnson had a paralytic stroke in June. Death was sending preliminary warnings. A correspondence was kept up, which implies that the old terms were not ostensibly broken. Mrs. Thrale speaks tartly more than once ; and Johnson's letters go into medical details with his customary plainness of speech, and he occasionally indulges in laments over the supposed change in her feelings. The gloom is thickening, and the old playful gallantry has died out. The old man evidently felt himself deserted, and suffered from the breaking-up of the asylum he had loved so well. The final catastrophe came in 1784, less than six months before Johnson's death.

After much suffering in mind and body, Mrs. Thrale had at last induced her daughters to consent to her marriage with Piozzi. She sent for him at once, and they were married in June, 1784. A painful correspondence followed. Mrs. Thrale announced her marriage in a friendly letter to Johnson, excusing her previous silence on the ground that discussion could only have caused them pain. The revelation, though Johnson could not have been quite unprepared, produced one of his bursts of fury. " Madam, if I interpret your letter rightly," wrote the old man, " you are ignominiously married. If it is yet undone, let us once more talk together. If you have abandoned your children and your religion, God forgive your wickedness ! If you have forfeited your fame and your country, may your folly do no further mischief ! If the last act is yet to do, I, who have loved you, esteemed

you, reverenced you, and served you—I, who long thought
you the first of womankind—entreat that before your fate
is irrevocable, I may once more see you! I was, I once
was, madam, most truly yours, Sam. Johnson."

Mrs. Thrale replied with spirit and dignity to this cry
of blind indignation, speaking of her husband with becoming pride, and resenting the unfortunate phrase about
her loss of "fame." She ended by declining further
intercourse till Johnson could change his opinion of
Piozzi. Johnson admitted in his reply that he had no
right to resent her conduct; expressed his gratitude for
the kindness which had " soothed twenty years of a life
radically wretched," and implored her (" superfluously," as
she says) to induce Piozzi to settle in England. He then
took leave of her with an expression of sad forebodings.
Mrs. Thrale, now Mrs. Piozzi, says that she replied affec-
tionately; but the letter is missing. The friendship was
broken off, and during the brief remainder of Johnson's
life, the Piozzis were absent from England.

Of her there is little more to be said. After passing
some time in Italy, where she became a light of that
wretched little Della Cruscan society of which some
faint memory is preserved by Gifford's ridicule, now pretty
nearly forgotten with its objects, she returned with her
husband to England. Her anecdotes of Johnson, published soon after his death, had a success which, in spite
of much ridicule, encouraged her to some further literary
efforts of a sprightly but ephemeral kind. She lived
happily with Piozzi, and never had cause to regret her
marriage. She was reconciled to her daughters sufficiently
to renew a friendly intercourse ; but the elder ones set up
a separate establishment. Piozzi died not long afterwards. She was still a vivacious old lady, who celebrated

her 80th birthday by a ball; and is supposed at that ripe age to have made an offer of marriage to a young actor. She died in May, 1821, leaving all that she could dispose of to a nephew of Piozzi's, who had been naturalised in England.

Meanwhile Johnson was rapidly approaching the grave. His old inmates, Levett and Miss Williams, had gone before him ; Goldsmith and Garrick and Beauclerk had become memories of the past; and the gloom gathered thickly around him. The old man clung to life with pathetic earnestness. Though life had been often melancholy, he never affected to conceal the horror with which he regarded death. He frequently declared that death must be dreadful to every reasonable man. "Death, my dear, is very dreadful," he says simply in a letter to Lucy Porter in the last year of his life. Still later he shocked a pious friend by admitting that the fear oppressed him. Dr. Adams tried the ordinary consolation of the divine goodness, and went so far as to suggest that hell might not imply much positive suffering. Johnson's religious views were of a different colour. " I am afraid," he said, " I may be one of those who shall be damned." " What do you mean by damned?" asked Adams. Johnson replied passionately and loudly, " Sent to hell, sir, and punished everlastingly." Remonstrances only deepened his melancholy, and he silenced his friends by exclaiming in gloomy agitation, " I'll have no more on't !" Often in these last years he was heard muttering to himself the passionate complaint of Claudio, " Ah, but to die and go we know not whither !" At other times he was speaking of some lost friend, and saying, " Poor man—and then he died !" The peculiar horror of death, which seems to indicate a tinge of insanity, was combined with utter

M

fearlessness of pain. He called to the surgeons to cut deeper when performing a painful operation, and shortly before his death inflicted such wounds upon himself in hopes of obtaining relief as, very erroneously, to suggest the idea of suicide. Whilst his strength remained, he endeavoured to disperse melancholy by some of the old methods. In the winter of 1783-4 he got together the few surviving members of the old Ivy Lane Club, which had flourished when he was composing the *Dictionary ;* but the old place of meeting had vanished, most of the original members were dead, and the gathering can have been but melancholy. He started another club at the Essex Head, whose members were to meet twice a week, with the modest fine of threepence for non-attendance. It appears to have included a rather " strange mixture " of people, and thereby to have given some scandal to Sir John Hawkins and even to Reynolds. They thought that his craving for society, increased by his loss of Streatham, was leading him to undignified concessions.

Amongst the members of the club, however, were such men as Horsley and Windham. Windham seems to have attracted more personal regard than most politicians, by a generous warmth of enthusiasm not too common in the class. In politics he was an ardent disciple of Burke's, whom he afterwards followed in his separation from the new Whigs. But, though adhering to the principles which Johnson detested, he knew, like his preceptor, how to win Johnson's warmest regard. He was the most eminent of the younger generation who now looked up to Johnson as a venerable relic from the past. Another was young Burke, that very priggish and silly young man as he seems to have been, whose loss, none the less, broke the tender heart of his father. Friendships, now more interesting, were those with two of the most distinguished authoresses of the day. One of them was Hannah More, who was about this time coming to the conclusion that the talents which had gained her distinction in the literary and even in the dramatic world, should be consecrated to less secular employment. Her vivacity during the earlier years of their acquaintance exposed her to an occasional rebuff. "She does not gain upon me, sir ; I think her empty-headed," was one of his remarks ; and it was to her that he said, according to Mrs. Thrale, though Boswell reports a softened version of the remark, that she should " consider what her flattery was worth, before she choked him with it." More frequently, he seems to have repaid it in kind. "There was no name in poetry," he said, "which might not be glad to own her poem"—the *Bas Bleu.* Certainly Johnson did not stick at trifles in intercourse with his female friends. He was delighted, shortly before his death, to " gallant it about" with her at Oxford, and in serious moments showed a respectful regard for her merits. Hannah More, who thus sat at the feet of Johnson, encouraged the juvenile ambition of Macaulay, and did not die till the historian had grown into manhood and fame. The other friendship noticed was with Fanny Burney, who also lived to our own time. Johnson's affection for this daughter of his friend seems to have been amongst the tenderest of his old age. When she was first introduced to him at the Thrales, she was overpowered and indeed had her head a little turned by flattery of the most agreeable kind that an author can receive. The " great literary Leviathan" showed himself to have the recently pub-lished *Evelina* at his fingers' ends. He quoted, and almost acted passages. " La ! Polly !" he exclaimed in a

pert feminine accent, " only think ! Miss has danced with
a lord ! " How many modern readers can assign its place
to that quotation, or answer the question which poor
Boswell asked in despair and amidst general ridicule for
his ignorance, " What is a Brangton ? " There is something pleasant in the enthusiasm with which men like
Johnson and Burke welcomed the literary achievements
of the young lady, whose first novels seem to have made
a sensation almost as lively as that produced by Miss
Brontë, and far superior to anything that fell to the lot
of Miss Austen. Johnson seems always to have regarded
her with personal affection. He had a tender interview
with her shortly before his death ; he begged her with
solemn energy to remember him in her prayers ; he
apologized pathetically for being unable to see her, as
his weakness increased ; and sent her tender messages
from his deathbed.

As the end drew near, Johnson accepted the inevitable
like a man. After spending most of the latter months of
1784 in the country with the friends who, after the loss of
the Thrales, could give him most domestic comfort, he came
back to London to die. He made his will, and settled a
few matters of business, and was pleased to be told that
he would be buried in Westminster Abbey. He uttered
a few words of solemn advice to those who came near
him, and took affecting leave of his friends. Langton,
so warmly loved, was in close attendance. Johnson said
to him tenderly, *Te teneam moriens deficiente manu.*
Windham broke from political occupations to sit by the
dying man. Once Langton found Burke sitting by his
bedside with three or four friends. "I am afraid," said
Burke, " that so many of us must be oppressive to you."
" No, sir, it is not so," replied Johnson, " and I must be

in a wretched state indeed when your company would not be a delight to me." "My dear sir," said Burke, with a breaking voice, "you have always been too good to me ;" and parted from his old friend for the last time. Of Reynolds, he begged three things : to forgive a debt of thirty pounds, to read the Bible, and never to paint on Sundays. A few flashes of the old humour broke through. He said of a man who sat up with him : " Sir, the fellow's an idiot; he's as awkward as a turnspit when first put into the wheel, and as sleepy as a dormouse," His last recorded words were to a young lady who had begged for his blessing : "God bless you, my dear." The same day, December 13th, 1784, he gradually sank and died peacefully. He was laid in the Abbey, and the playful prediction which he made to Goldsmith has been amply fulfilled :—

Forsitan et nostrum nomen miscebitur istis.

The names of many greater writers are inscribed upon the walls of Westminster Abbey ; but scarcely any one lies there whose heart was more acutely responsive during life to the deepest and tenderest of human emotions. In visiting that strange gathering of departed heroes and statesmen and philanthropists and poets, there are many whose words and deeds have a far greater influence upon our imaginations ; but there are very few whom, when all has been said, we can love so heartily as Samuel Johnson.

CHAPTER VI.

JOHNSON'S WRITINGS.

IT remains to speak of Johnson's position in literature. For reasons sufficiently obvious, few men whose lives have been devoted to letters for an equal period, have left behind them such scanty and inadequate remains. John-son, as we have seen, worked only under the pressure of circumstances; a very small proportion of his latter life was devoted to literary employment. The working hours of his earlier years were spent for the most part in pro-ductions which can hardly be called literary. Seven years were devoted to the *Dictionary*, which, whatever its merits, could be a book only in the material sense of the word, and was of course destined to be soon superseded. Much of his hack-work has doubtless passed into oblivion, and though the ordinary relic-worship has gathered together fragments enough to fill twelve decent octavo volumes (to which may be added the two volumes of parliamentary reports), the part which can be called alive may be compressed into very moderate compass. Johnson may be considered as a poet, an essayist, a pamphleteer, a traveller, a critic, and a biographer. Among his poems, the two imitations of Juvenal, especially the *Vanity of Human Wishes*, and a minor fragment or two, probably deserve more respect than would be conceded to them by adherents of modern schools. His most ambitious work, *Irene*, can be read by men in whom a sense of duty has been abnormally developed. Among the two hundred and odd essays of the *Rambler*, there is a fair proportion which will deserve, but will hardly obtain, respectful attention. *Rasselas*, one of the philosophical tales popular in the last century, gives the essence of much of the *Rambler* in a different form, and to these may be added the essay upon Soame Jenyns, which deals with the same absorbing question of human happiness. The political pamphlets, and the *Journey to the Hebrides*, have a certain historical interest; but are otherwise readable only in particular passages. Much of his criticism is pretty nearly obsolete; but the child of his old age—the *Lives of the Poets*—a book in which criticism and biography are combined, is an admirable performance in spite of serious defects. It is the work that best reflects his mind, and intelligent readers who have once made its acquaintance, will be apt to turn it into a familiar companion.

If it is easy to assign the causes which limited the quantity of Johnson's work, it is more curious to inquire what was the quality which once gained for it so much authority, and which now seems to have so far lost its savour. The peculiar style which is associated with Johnson's name must count for something in both processes. The mannerism is strongly marked, and of course offensive; for by "mannerism," as I understand the word, is meant the repetition of certain forms of language in obedience to blind habit and without reference to their propriety in the particular case. Johnson's sentences seem to be contorted, as his gigantic limbs used to twitch, by a kind of mechanical spasmodic action. The most obvious peculiarity is the tendency which he noticed himself, to "use too big words and too many of them." He had to explain to Miss Reynolds that the Shakesperian line,—

You must borrow me Garagantua's mouth,

had been applied to him because he used "big words, which require the mouth of a giant to pronounce them." It was not, however, the mere bigness of the words that distinguished his style, but a peculiar love of putting the abstract for the concrete, of using awkward inversions, and of balancing his sentences in a monotonous rhythm, which gives the appearance, as it sometimes corresponds to the reality, of elaborate logical discrimination. With all its faults the style has the merits of masculine directness. The inversions are not such as to complicate the construction. As Boswell remarks, he never uses a parenthesis; and his style, though ponderous and wearisome, is as transparent as the smarter snip-snap of Macaulay.

This singular mannerism appears in his earliest writings; it is most marked at the time of the *Rambler;* whilst in the *Lives of the Poets,* although I think that the trick of inversion has become commoner, the other peculiarities have been so far softened as (in my judgment, at least), to be inoffensive. It is perhaps needless to give examples of a tendency which marks almost every page of his writing. A passage or two from the *Rambler* may illustrate the quality of the style, and the oddity of the effect produced, when it is applied to topics of a trivial kind. The author of the *Rambler* is supposed to receive a remonstrance upon his excessive gravity from the lively Flirtilla, who wishes him to write in defence of masquerades. Conscious of his own incapacity, he applies to a man of "high reputation in gay life ;" who, on the fifth perusal of Flirtilla's letter breaks into a rapture, and declares that he is ready to devote himself to her service. Here is part of the apostrophe put into the mouth of this brilliant rake. "Behold, Flirtilla, at thy feet a man grown gray in the study of those noble arts by which right and wrong may be confounded; by which reason may be blinded, when we have a mind to escape from her inspection, and caprice and appetite instated in uncontrolled command and boundless dominion! Such a casuist may surely engage with certainty of success in vindication of an entertainment which in an instant gives confidence to the timorous and kindles ardour in the cold, an entertainment where the vigilance of jealousy has so often been clouded, and the virgin is set free from the necessity of languishing in silence ; where all the outworks of chastity are at once demolished; where the heart is laid open without a blush ; where bashfulness may survive virtue, and no wish is crushed under the frown of modesty."

Here is another passage, in which Johnson is speaking upon a topic more within his proper province ; and which contains sound sense under its weight of words. A man, he says, who reads a printed book, is often contented to be pleased without critical examination. "But," he adds, "if the same man be called to consider the merit of a production yet unpublished, he brings an imagination heated with objections to passages which he has never yet heard; he invokes all the powers of criticism, and stores his memory with Taste and Grace, Purity and Delicacy, Manners and Unities, sounds which having been once uttered by those that understood

them, have been since re-echoed without meaning, and
kept up to the disturbance of the world by constant
repercussion from one coxcomb to another. He considers himself as obliged to show by some proof of his
abilities, that he is not consulted to no purpose, and
therefore watches every opening for objection, and looks
round for every opportunity to propose some specious
alteration. Such opportunities a very small degree of
sagacity will enable him to find, for in every work of
imagination, the disposition of parts, the insertion of
incidents, and use of decorations may be varied in a
thousand ways with equal propriety ; and, as in things
nearly equal that will always seem best to every man
which he himself produces, the critic, whose business
is only to propose without the care of execution, can
never want the satisfaction of believing that he has
suggested very important improvements, nor the power
of enforcing his advice by arguments, which, as they
appear convincing to himself, either his kindness or his
vanity will press obstinately and importunately, without
suspicion that he may possibly judge too hastily in favour
of his own advice or inquiry whether the advantage of
the new scheme be proportionate to the labour." We may
still notice a "repercussion" of words from one coxcomb
to another ; though somehow the words have been
changed or translated.

Johnson's style is characteristic of the individual and
of the epoch. The preceding generation had exhibited
the final triumph of common sense over the pedantry of a
decaying scholasticism. The movements represented by
Locke's philosophy, by the rationalizing school in theology,
and by the so-called classicism of Pope and his followers,
are different phases of the same impulse. The quality

valued above all others in philosophy, literature, and art was clear, bright, common sense. To expel the mystery which had served as a cloak for charlatans was the great aim of the time, and the method was to appeal from the professors of exploded technicalities to the judgment of cultivated men of the world. Berkeley places his Utopia in happy climes, —

> Where nature guides, and virtue rules,
> *Where men shall not impose for truth and sense*
> *The pedantry of courts and schools.*

Simplicity, clearness, directness are, therefore, the great virtues of thought and style. Berkeley, Addison, Pope, and Swift are the great models of such excellence in various departments of literature.

In the succeeding generation we become aware of a certain leaven of dissatisfaction with the æsthetic and intellectual code thus inherited. The supremacy of common sense, the superlative importance of clearness, is still fully acknowledged, but there is a growing undertone of dissent in form and substance. Attempts are made to restore philosophical conceptions assailed by Locke and his followers; the rationalism of the deistic or semi-deistic writers is declared to be superficial; their optimistic theories disregard the dark side of nature, and provide no sufficient utterance for the sadness caused by the contemplation of human suffering; and the polished monotony of Pope's verses begins to fall upon those who shall tread in his steps. Some daring sceptics are even inquiring whether he is a poet at all. And simultaneously, though Addison is still a kind of sacred model, the best prose writers are beginning to aim at a more complex structure of sentence, fitted for the expression of a wider range of thought and emotion.

Johnson, though no conscious revolutionist, shares this growing discontent. The *Spectator* is written in the language of the drawing-room and the coffee-house. Nothing is ever said which might not pass in conversation between a couple of "wits," with, at most, some graceful indulgence in passing moods of solemn or tender sentiment. Johnson, though devoted to society in his own way, was anything but a producer of small talk. Society meant to him an escape from the gloom which beset him whenever he was abandoned to his thoughts. Neither his education nor the manners acquired in Grub Street had qualified him to be an observer of those lighter foibles which were touched by Addison with so dexterous a hand. When he ventures upon such topics he flounders dreadfully, and rather reminds us of an artist who should attempt to paint miniatures with a mop. No man, indeed, took more of interest in what is called the science of human nature ; and, when roused by the stimulus of argument, he could talk, as has been shown, with almost unrivalled vigour and point. But his favourite topics are the deeper springs of character, rather than superficial peculiarities ; and his vigorous sayings are concentrated essence of strong sense and deep feeling, not dainty epigrams or graceful embodiments of delicate observation. Johnson was not, like some contemporary antiquarians, a systematic student of the English literature of the preceding centuries, but he had a strong affection for some of its chief masterpieces. Burton's *Anatomy of Melancholy* was, he declared, the only book which ever got him out of bed two hours sooner than he wished. Sir Thomas Browne was another congenial writer, who is supposed to have had some influence upon his style. He never seems to have directly imitated any one, though some nonsense has been talked about his "forming a style;" but it is probable that he felt a closer affinity to those old scholars, with their elaborate and ornate language and their deep and solemn tone of sentiment, than to the brilliant but comparatively superficial writers of Queen Anne's time. He was, one may say, a scholar of the old type, forced by circumstances upon the world, but always retaining a sympathy for the scholar's life and temper. Accordingly, his style acquired something of the old elaboration, though the attempt to conform to the canons of a later age renders the structure disagreeably monotonous. His tendency to pomposity is not redeemed by the *naïveté* and spontaneity of his masters.

The inferiority of Johnson's written to his spoken utterances is indicative of his divided life. There are moments at which his writing takes the terse, vigorous tone of his talk. In his letters, such as those to Chesterfield and Macpherson and in occasional passages of his pamphlets, we see that he could be pithy enough when he chose to descend from his Latinized abstractions to good concrete English; but that is only when he becomes excited. His face when in repose, we are told, appeared to be almost imbecile; he was constantly sunk in reveries, from which he was only roused by a challenge to conversation. In his writings, for the most part, we seem to be listening to the reverie rather than the talk; we are overhearing a soliloquy in his study, not a vigorous discussion over the twentieth cup of tea; he is not fairly put upon his mettle, and is content to expound without enforcing. We seem to see a man, heavy-eyed, ponderous in his gestures, like some huge mechanism which grinds out a ponderous tissue of verbiage as heavy as it is certainly solid.

The substance corresponds to the style. Johnson has

something in common with the fashionable pessimism of
modern times.   No sentimentalist of to-day could be more
convinced that life is in the main miserable.   It was his
favourite theory, according to Mrs. Thrale, that all human
action was prompted by the " vacuity of life."   Men act
solely in the hope of escaping from themselves.   Evil, as
a follower of Schopenhauer would assert, is the positive,
and good merely the negative of evil.   All desire is at
bottom an attempt to escape from pain.   The doctrine
neither resulted from, nor generated, a philosophical theory
in Johnson's case, and was in the main a generaliza-
tion of his own experience.   Not the less, the aim of
most of his writing is to express this sentiment in one
form or other.   He differs, indeed, from most modern
sentimentalists, in having the most hearty contempt for
useless whining.   If he dwells upon human misery, it is
because he feels that it is as futile to join with the optimist in ignoring, as with the pessimist in howling over
the evil.   We are in a sad world, full of pain, but
we have to make the best of it.   Stubborn patience and
hard work are the sole remedies, or rather the sole
means of temporary escape.   Much of the *Rambler* is
occupied with variations upon this theme, and expresses
the kind of dogged resolution with which he would have
us plod through this weary world.   Take for example
this passage :—" The controversy about the reality of
external evils is now at an end.   That life has many
miseries, and that those miseries are sometimes at least
equal to all the powers of fortitude is now universally
confessed ; and, therefore, it is useful to consider not only
how we may escape them, but by what means those
which either the accidents of affairs or the infirmities
of nature must bring upon us may be mitigated and

lightened, and how we may make those hours less wretched which the condition of our present existence will not allow to be very happy.

" The cure for the greatest part of human miseries is not radical, but palliative. Infelicity is involved in corporeal nature, and interwoven with our being; all attempts, therefore, to decline it wholly are useless and vain ; the armies of pàin send their arrows against us on every side, the choice is only between those which are more or less sharp, or tinged with poison of greater or less malignity ; and the strongest armour which reason can supply will only blunt their points, but cannot repel them.

"The great remedy which Heaven has put in our hands is patience, by which, though we cannot lessen the torments of the body, we can in a great measure preserve the peace of the mind, and shall suffer only the natural and genuine force of an evil, without heightening its acrimony or prolonging its effects."

It is hardly desirable for a moralist to aim at originality in his precepts. We must be content if he enforces old truths in such a manner as to convince us of the depth and sincerity of his feeling. Johnson, it must be confessed, rather abuses the moralist's privilege of being commonplace. He descants not unfrequently upon propositions so trite that even the most earnest enforcement can give them little interest. With all drawbacks, however, the moralizing is the best part of the *Rambler*. Many of the papers follow the precedent set by Addison in the *Spectator*, but without Addison's felicity. Like Addison, he indulges in allegory, which, in his hands, becomes unendurably frigid and clumsy ; he tries light social satire, and is fain to confess that we can spy a beard under the muffler of his feminine characters ; he

treats us to criticism which, like Addison's, goes upon
exploded principles, but unlike Addison's, is apt to be
almost wilfully outrageous.   His odd remarks upon
Milton's versification are the worst example of this weakness.   The result is what one might expect from the
attempt of a writer without an ear to sit in judgment
upon the greatest master of harmony in the language.

These defects have consigned the *Rambler* to the
dustiest shelves of libraries, and account for the wonder
expressed by such a critic as M. Taine at the English
love of Johnson.   Certainly if that love were nourished,
as he seems to fancy, by assiduous study of the *Rambler*,
it would be a curious phenomenon.   And yet with all
its faults, the reader who can plod through its pages
will at least feel respect for the author.   It is not
unworthy of the man whose great lesson is " clear your
mind of cant ;"[1] who felt most deeply the misery of the
world, but from the bottom of his heart despised
querulous and sentimental complaints on one side, and
optimist glasses upon the other.   To him, as to some others
of his temperament, the affectation of looking at the
bright side of things seems to have presented itself as the
bitterest of mockeries ; and nothing would tempt him
to let fine words pass themselves off for genuine sense.
Here are some remarks upon the vanity in which some
authors seek for consolation, which may illustrate this

---

[1] Of this well-known sentiment it may be said, as of some other
familiar quotations, that its direct meaning has been slightly
modified in use.   The emphasis is changed.   Johnson's words
were " Clear your *mind* of cant.   You may talk as other people do ;
you may say to a man, sir, I am your humble servant ; you are *not*
his most humble servant. . . .   You may *talk* in this manner ;
it is a mode of talking in society ; but don't *think* foolishly."

love of realities and conclude our quotations from the *Rambler*.

"By such acts of voluntary delusion does every man endeavour to conceal his own unimportance from himself. It is long before we are convinced of the small proportion which every individual bears to the collective body of mankind; or learn how few can be interested in the fortune of any single man; how little vacancy is left in the world for any new object of attention; to how small extent the brightest blaze of merit can be spread amidst the mists of business and of folly; and how soon it is clouded by the intervention of other novelties. Not only the writer of books, but the commander of armies, and the deliverer of nations, will easily outlive all noisy and popular reputation: he may be celebrated for a time by the public voice, but his actions and his name will soon be considered as remote and unaffecting, and be rarely mentioned but by those whose alliance gives them some vanity to gratify by frequent commemoration. It seems not to be sufficiently considered how little renown can be admitted in the world. Mankind are kept perpetually busy by their fears or desires, and have not more leisure from their own affairs than to acquaint themselves with the accidents of the current day. Engaged in contriving some refuge from calamity, or in shortening their way to some new possession, they seldom suffer their thoughts to wander to the past or future; none but a few solitary students have leisure to inquire into the claims of ancient heroes or sages; and names which hoped to range over kingdoms and continents shrink at last into cloisters and colleges. Nor is it certain that even of these dark and narrow habitations, these last retreats of fame, the possession will be long kept. Of men devoted

N

to literature very few extend their views beyond some
particular science, and the greater part seldom inquire, even
in their own profession, for any authors but those whom
the present mode of study happens to force upon their
notice ; they desire not to fill their minds with un-
fashionable knowledge, but contentedly resign to oblivion
those books which they now find censured or neglected."

The most remarkable of Johnson's utterances upon
his favourite topic of the Vanity of Human Wishes is
the story of *Rasselas*. The plan of the book is simple,
and recalls certain parts of Voltaire's simultaneous but
incomparably more brilliant attack upon Optimism in
Candide. There is supposed to be a happy valley in
Abyssinia where the royal princes are confined in total
seclusion, but with ample supplies for every conceivable
want. Rasselas, who has been thus educated, becomes
curious as to the outside world, and at last makes his
escape with his sister, her attendant, and the ancient
sage and poet, Imlac. Under Imlac's guidance they
survey life and manners in various stations; they make
the acquaintance of philosophers, statesmen, men of the
world, and recluses ; they discuss the results of their
experience pretty much in the style of the *Rambler ;*
they agree to pronounce the sentence "Vanity of
Vanities ! " and finally, in a "conclusion where nothing is
concluded," they resolve to return to the happy valley.
The book is little more than a set of essays upon life,
with just story enough to hold it together. It is wanting in those brilliant flashes of epigram, which illustrate
Voltaire's pages so as to blind some readers to its real
force of sentiment, and yet it leaves a peculiar and
powerful impression upon the reader.

The general tone may be collected from a few passages.

Here is a fragment, the conclusion of which is perhaps the most familiar of quotations from Johnson's writings. Imlac in narrating his life describes his attempts to become a poet.

" The business of a poet," said Imlac, " is to examine not the individual, but the species; to remark general properties and large appearances; he does not number the streaks of the tulip or describe the different shades in the verdure of the forest. He is to exhibit in his portraits of nature such prominent and striking features as recall the original to every mind; and must neglect the minute discriminations which one may have remarked, and another have neglected for those characteristics which are alike obvious to vigilance and carelessness."

" But the knowledge of nature is only half the task of a poet; he must be acquainted likewise with all the modes of life. His character requires that he estimate the happiness and misery of every condition; observe the power of all the passions in all their combinations, and know the changes of the human mind as they are modified by various institutions, and accidental influences of climate or custom, from the sprightliness of infancy to the despondency of decrepitude. He must divest himself of the prejudices of his age or country; he must consider right and wrong in their abstracted and invariable state; he must disregard present laws and opinions, and rise to general and transcendental truths, which will always be the same; he must therefore content himself with the slow progress of his name; contemn the applause of his own time, and commit his claims to the justice of posterity. He must write as the interpreter of nature and the legislator of mankind, and consider himself as presiding over the thoughts and manners of future generations, as a being superior to time and place.

"His labours are not yet at an end; he must know many languages and many sciences; and that his style may be worthy of his thoughts, must by incessant practice familiarize to himself every delicacy of speech and grace of harmony."

Imlac now felt the enthusiastic fit and was proceeding to aggrandize his profession, when the prince cried out, "Enough, thou hast convinced me that no human being can ever be a poet."

Indeed, Johnson's conception of poetry is not the one which is now fashionable, and which would rather seem to imply that philosophical power and moral sensibility are so far disqualifications to the true poet.

Here, again, is a view of the superfine system of moral philosophy. A meeting of learned men is discussing the ever-recurring problem of happiness, and one of them speaks as follows :—

"The way to be happy is to live according to nature, in obedience to that universal and unalterable law with which every heart is originally impressed; which is not written on it by precept, but engraven by destiny, not instilled by education, but infused at our nativity. He that lives according to nature will suffer nothing from the delusions of hope, or importunities of desire; he will receive and reject with equability of temper, and act or suffer as the reason of things shall alternately prescribe. Other men may amuse themselves with subtle definitions or intricate ratiocinations. Let him learn to be wise by easier means : let him observe the hind of the forest, and the linnet of the grove; let him consider the life of animals whose motions are regulated by instinct; they obey their guide and are happy.

"Let us, therefore, at length cease to dispute, and learn to live; throw away the incumbrance of precepts, which they who utter them with so much pride and pomp do not understand, and carry with us this simple and intelligible maxim, that deviation from nature is deviation from happiness."

The prince modestly inquires what is the precise meaning of the advice just given.

"When I find young men so humble and so docile," said the philosopher, "I can deny them no information which my studies have enabled me to afford. To live according to nature, is to act always with due regard to the fitness arising from the relations and qualities of causes and effects, to concur with the great and unchangeable scheme of universal felicity; to co-operate with the general disposition and tendency of the present system of things.

"The prince soon found that this was one of the sages, whom he should understand less as he heard him longer."

Here, finally, is a characteristic reflection upon the right mode of meeting sorrow.

"The state of a mind oppressed with a sudden calamity," said Imlac, "is like that of the fabulous inhabitants of the new created earth, who, when the first night came upon them, supposed that day would never return. When the clouds of sorrow gather over us, we see nothing beyond them, nor can imagine how they will be dispelled; yet a new day succeeded to the night, and sorrow is never long without a dawn of ease. But as they who restrain themselves from receiving comfort, do

as the savages would have done, had they put out their
eyes when it was dark. Our minds, like our bodies, are
in continual flux ; something is hourly lost, and something acquired. To lose much at once is inconvenient to
either, but while the vital powers remain uninjured,
nature will find the means of reparation.

"Distance has the same effect on the mind as on the
eye, and while we glide along the stream of time, whatever we leave behind us is always lessening, and that
which we approach increasing in magnitude. Do not
suffer life to stagnate ; it will grow muddy for want of
motion ; commit yourself again to the current of the
world ; Pekuah will vanish by degrees ; you will meet in
your way some other favourite, or learn to diffuse yourself in general conversation."

In one respect *Rasselas* is curiously contrasted with
Candide. Voltaire's story is aimed at the doctrine of
theological optimism, and, whether that doctrine be well
or ill understood, has therefore an openly sceptical tendency. Johnson, to whom nothing could be more abhorrent than an alliance with any assailant of orthodoxy,
draws no inference from his pessimism. He is content to
state the fact of human misery without perplexing himself with the resulting problem as to the final cause of
human existence. If the question had been explicitly
brought before him, he would, doubtless, have replied
that the mystery was insoluble. To answer either in the
sceptical or the optimistic sense was equally presumptuous.
Johnson's religious beliefs in fact were not such as to suggest that kind of comfort which is to be obtained by explain-
ing away the existence of evil. If he, too, would have
said that in some sense all must be for the best in a world
ruled by a perfect Creator, the sense must be one which

would allow of the eternal misery of indefinite multitudes
of his creatures.

But, in truth, it was characteristic of Johnson to turn
away his mind from such topics. He was interested in
ethical speculations, but on the practical side, in the
application to life, not in the philosophy on which it
might be grounded. In that direction he could see
nothing but a " milking of the bull "—a fruitless or
rather a pernicious waste of intellect. An intense conviction of the supreme importance of a moral guidance in
this difficult world, made him abhor any rash inquiries by
which the basis of existing authority might be endangered.

This sentiment is involved in many of those prejudices
which have been so much, and in some sense justifiably
ridiculed. Man has been wretched and foolish since the
race began, and will be till it ends ; one chorus of lamen-
tation has ever been rising, in countless dialects but with
a single meaning ; the plausible schemes of philosophers
give no solution to the everlasting riddle ; the nostrums
of politicians touch only the surface of the deeply-rooted
evil ; it is folly to be querulous, and as silly to fancy that
men are growing worse, as that they are much better than
they used to be. The evils under which we suffer are
not skin-deep, to be eradicated by changing the old physicians for new quacks. What is to be done under such
conditions, but to hold fast as vigorously as we can to the
rules of life and faith which have served our ancestors,
and which, whatever their justifications, are at least the
only consolation, because they supply the only guidance
through this labyrinth of troubles ? Macaulay has ridiculed Johnson for what he takes to be the ludicrous in-
consistency of his intense political prejudice, combined
with his assertion of the indifference of all forms of

government. "If," says Macaulay, "the difference between two forms of government be not worth half a
guinea, it is not easy to see how Whiggism can be viler
than Toryism, or the Crown can have too little power."
The answer is surely obvious. Whiggism is vile,
according to the doctor's phrase, because Whiggism is a
"negation of all principle;" it is in his view, not so
much the preference of one form to another, as an attack
upon the vital condition of all government. He called
Burke a "bottomless Whig" in this sense, implying that
Whiggism meant anarchy; and in the next generation
a good many people were led, rightly or wrongly, to agree
with him by the experience of the French revolution.

This dogged conservatism has both its value and its
grotesque side. When Johnson came to write political
pamphlets in his later years, and to deal with subjects
little familiar to his mind, the results were grotesque
enough. Loving authority, and holding one authority to
be as good as another, he defended with uncompromising
zeal the most preposterous and tyrannical measures.
The pamphlets against the Wilkite agitators and the
American rebels are little more than a huge "rhinoceros"
snort of contempt against all who are fools enough or
wicked enough to promote war and disturbance in order to
change one form of authority for another. Here is a
characteristic passage, giving his view of the value of
such demonstrators:—

"The progress of a petition is well known. An ejected
placeman goes down to his county or his borough, tells
his friends of his inability to serve them and his consti-
tuents, of the corruption of the government. His friends
readily understand that he who can get nothing, will have
nothing to give. They agree to proclaim a meeting.

Meat and drink are plentifully provided, a crowd is easily brought together, and those who think that they know the reason of the meeting undertake to tell those who know it not. Ale and clamour unite their powers; the crowd, condensed and heated, begins to ferment with the leaven of sedition. All see a thousand evils, though they cannot show them, and grow impatient for a remedy, though they know not what.

"A speech is then made by the Cicero of the day; he says much and suppresses more, and credit is equally given to what he tells and what he conceals. The petition is heard and universally approved. Those who are sober enough to write, add their names, and the rest would sign it if they could.

"Every man goes home and tells his neighbour of the glories of the day; how he was consulted, and what he advised; how he was invited into the great room, where his lordship caressed him by his name; how he was caressed by Sir Francis, Sir Joseph, and Sir George; how he ate turtle and venison, and drank unanimity to the three brothers.

"The poor loiterer, whose shop had confined him or whose wife had locked him up, hears the tale of luxury with envy, and at last inquires what was their petition. Of the petition nothing is remembered by the narrator, but that it spoke much of fears and apprehensions and something very alarming, but that he is sure it is against the government.

"The other is convinced that it must be right, and wishes he had been there, for he loves wine and venison, and resolves as long as he lives to be against the government.

"The petition is then handed from town to town, and from house to house; and wherever it comes, the inha-

bitants flock together that they may see that which must
be sent to the king. Names are easily collected. One
man signs because he hates the papists; another because
he has vowed destruction to the turnpikes; one because
it will vex the parson; another because he owes his land-
lord nothing; one because he is rich; another because he
is poor; one to show that he is not afraid; and another
to show that he can write."

The only writing in which we see a distinct reflection
of Johnson's talk is the *Lives of the Poets*. The excellence
of that book is of the same kind as the excellence of his
conversation. Johnson wrote it under pressure, and it has
suffered from his characteristic indolence. Modern authors
would fill as many pages as Johnson has filled lines, with
the biographies of some of his heroes. By industriously
sweeping together all the rubbish which is in any way
connected with the great man, by elaborately discussing
the possible significance of infinitesimal bits of evidence,
and by disquisition upon general principles or the whole
mass of contemporary literature, it is easy to swell volumes
to any desired extent. The result is sometimes highly
interesting and valuable, as it is sometimes a new contri-
bution to the dust-heaps; but in any case the design is
something quite different from Johnson's. He has left
much to be supplied and corrected by later scholars. His
aim is simply to give a vigorous summary of the main
facts of his heroes' lives, a pithy analysis of their character, and a short criticism of their productions. The
strong sense which is everywhere displayed, the massive
style, which is yet easier and less cumbrous than in his
earlier work, and the uprightness and independence of
the judgments, make the book agreeable even where we
are most inclined to dissent from its conclusions.

The criticism is that of a school which has died out under the great revolution of modern taste. The booksellers decided that English poetry began for their purposes with Cowley, and Johnson has, therefore, nothing to say about some of the greatest names in our literature. The loss is little to be regretted, since the biographical part of earlier memoirs must have been scanty, and the criticism inappreciative. Johnson, it may be said, like most of his contemporaries, considered poetry almost exclusively from the didactic and logical point of view. He always inquires what is the moral of a work of art. If he does not precisely ask " what it proves," he pays excessive attention to the logical solidity and coherence of its sentiments. He condemns not only insincerity and affectation of feeling, but all such poetic imagery as does not correspond to the actual prosaic belief of the writer. For the purely musical effects of poetry he has little or no feeling, and allows little deviation from the alternate long and short syllables neatly bound in Pope's couplets.

To many readers this would imply that Johnson omits precisely the poetic element in poetry. I must be here content to say that in my opinion it implies rather a limitation than a fundamental error. Johnson errs in supposing that his logical tests are at all adequate ; but it is, I think, a still greater error to assume that poetry has no connexion, because it has not this kind of connexion, with philosophy. His criticism has always a meaning, and in the case of works belonging to his own school a very sound meaning. When he is speaking of other poetry, we can only reply that his remarks may be true, but that they are not to the purpose.

The remarks on the poetry of Dryden, Addison, and Pope are generally excellent, and always give the genuine

expression of an independent judgment. Whoever thinks
for himself, and says plainly what he thinks, has some
merit as a critic. This, it is true, is about all that can be
said for such criticism as that on *Lycidas*, which is a
delicious example of the wrong way of applying strong
sense to inappropriate topics. Nothing can be truer in
a sense, and nothing less relevant.

"In this poem," he says, "there is no nature, for there
is no truth; there is no art, for there is nothing new. Its
form is that of a pastoral, easy, vulgar, and therefore dis-
gusting; whatever images it can supply are easily exhausted, and its inherent improbability always forces
dissatisfaction on the mind. When Cowley tells of
Hervey that they studied together, it is easy to suppose
how much he must miss the companion of his labours and
the partner of his discoveries; but what image of tenderness can be excited by these lines?—

> We drove afield, and both together heard
> What time the gray fly winds her sultry horn,
> Battening our flocks with the fresh dews of night.

We know that they never drove a-field and had no flocks
to batten; and though it be allowed that the representation may be allegorical, the true meaning is so uncertain
and remote that it is never sought, because it cannot be
known when it is found.

"Among the flocks and copses and flowers appear the
heathen deities : Jove and Phœbus, Neptune and Æolus,
with a long train of mythological imagery such as a college
easily supplies. Nothing can less display knowledge or
less exercise invention than to tell how a shepherd has
lost his companion, and must now feed his flocks alone,
without any judge of his skill in piping; how one god

asks another god what has become of Lycidas, and neither god can tell. He who thus grieves will excite no sympathy ; he who thus praises will confer no honour."

This is of course utterly outrageous, and yet much of it is undeniably true. To explain why, in spite of truth, *Lycidas* is a wonderful poem, would be to go pretty deeply into the theory of poetic expression. Most critics prefer simply to shriek, being at any rate safe from the errors of independent judgment.

The general effect of the book, however, is not to be inferred from this or some other passages of antiquated and eccentric criticism. It is the shrewd sense everywhere cropping up which is really delightful. The keen remarks upon life and character, though, perhaps, rather too severe in tone, are worthy of a vigorous mind, stored with much experience of many classes, and braced by constant exercise in the conversational arena. Passages everywhere abound which, though a little more formal in expression, have the forcible touch of his best conversational sallies. Some of the prejudices, which are expressed more pithily in *Boswell*, are defended by a reasoned exposition in the *Lives*. Sentence is passed with the true judicial air ; and if he does not convince us of his complete impartiality, he at least bases his decisions upon solid and worthy grounds. It would be too much, for example, to expect that Johnson should sympathize with the grand republicanism of Milton, or pardon a man who defended the execution of the blessed Martyr. He failed, therefore, to satisfy the ardent admirers of the great poet. Yet his judgment is not harsh or ungenerous, but, at worst, the judgment of a man striving to be just, in spite of some inevitable want of sympathy.

The quality of Johnson's incidental remarks may be

inferred from one or two brief extracts. Here is an observation which Johnson must have had many chances of verifying. Speaking of Dryden's money difficulties, he says, "It is well known that he seldom lives frugally who lives by chance. Hope is always liberal, and they that trust her promises, make little scruple of revelling to-day on the profits of the morrow."

Here is another shrewd comment upon the compliments paid to Halifax, of whom Pope says in the character of Bufo,—

> Fed with soft dedications all day long,
> Horace and he went hand and hand in song.

"To charge all unmerited praise with the guilt of flattery, or to suppose that the encomiast always knows and feels the falsehoods of his assertions, is surely to discover great ignorance of human nature and of human life. In determinations depending not on rules, but on reference and comparison, judgment is always in some degree subject to affection. Very near to admiration is the wish to admire.

"Every man willingly gives value to the praise which he receives, and considers the sentence passed in his favour as the sentence of discernment. We admire in a friend that understanding that selected us for confidence; we admire more in a patron that bounty which, instead of scattering bounty indiscriminately, directed it to us; and if the patron be an author, those performances which gratitude forbids us to blame, affection will easily dispose us to exalt.

"To these prejudices, hardly culpable, interest adds a power always operating, though not always, because not willingly, perceived. The modesty of praise gradually wears away; and, perhaps, the pride of patronage may be in time so increased that modest praise will no longer please.

"Many a blandishment was practised upon Halifax, which he would never have known had he no other attractions than those of his poetry, of which a short time has withered the beauties. It would now be esteemed no honour by a contributor to the monthly bundles of verses, to be told that, in strains either familiar or solemn, he sings like Halifax."

I will venture to make a longer quotation from the life of Pope, which gives, I think, a good impression of his manner :—

"Of his social qualities, if an estimate be made from his letters, an opinion too favourable cannot easily be formed ; they exhibit a perpetual and unclouded effulgence of general benevolence and particular fondness. There is nothing but liberality, gratitude, constancy, and tenderness. It has been so long said as to be commonly believed, that the true characters of men may be found in their letters, and that he who writes to his friend lays his heart open before him.

"But the truth is, that such were the simple friendships of the Golden Age, and are now the friendships only of children. Very few can boast of hearts which they dare lay open to themselves, and of which, by whatever accident exposed, they do not shun a distinct and continued view ; and certainly what we hide from ourselves, we do not show to our friends. There is, indeed, no transaction which offers stronger temptations to fallacy and sophistication than epistolary intercourse.

"In the eagerness of conversation, the first emotions of the mind often burst out before they are considered. In the tumult of business, interest and passion have their genuine effect ; but a friendly letter is a calm and deliberate performance in the cool of leisure, in the stillness of solitude, and surely no man sits down by design to depreciate his own character.

" Friendship has no tendency to secure veracity ; for by whom can a man so much wish to be thought better than he is, as by him whose kindness he desires to gain or keep ? Even in writing to the world there is less constraint ; the author is not confronted with his reader, and takes his chance of approbation among the different dispositions of mankind ; but a letter is addressed to a single mind, of which the prejudices and partialities are known, and must therefore please, if not by favouring them, by forbearing to oppose them. To charge those favourable representations which men give of their own minds, with the guilt of hypocritical falsehood, would show more severity than knowledge. The writer commonly believes himself. Almost every man's thoughts while they are general are right, and most hearts are pure while temptation is away. It is easy to awaken generous sentiments in privacy ; to despise death when there is no danger; to glow with benevolence when there is nothing to be given. While such ideas are formed they are felt, and self-love does not suspect the gleam of virtue to be the meteor of fancy.

" If the letters of Pope are considered merely as compositions, they seem to be premeditated and artificial. It is one thing to write, because there is something which the mind wishes to discharge ; and another to solicit the imagination, because ceremony or vanity requires something to be written. Pope confesses his early letters to be vitiated with *affectation and ambition.* To know whether he disentangles himself from these perverters of epistolary integrity, his book and his life must be set in comparison. One of his favourite topics is contempt of his own poetry. For this, if it had been real, he would deserve no commendation; and in this he was certainly not sincere, for his high value of himself was sufficiently observed; and of what could he be proud but of his poetry? He writes, he says, when 'he has just nothing else to do,' yet Swift complains that he was never at leisure for conversation, because he 'had always some poetical scheme in his head.' It was punctually required that his writing-box should be set upon his bed before he rose; and Lord Oxford's domestic related that, in the dreadful winter of '40, she was called from her bed by him four times in one night, to supply him with paper lest he should lose a thought.

"He pretends insensibility to censure and criticism, though it was observed by all who knew him that every pamphlet disturbed his quiet, and that his extreme irritability laid him open to perpetual vexation; but he wished to despise his critics, and therefore hoped he did despise them. As he happened to live in two reigns when the court paid little attention to poetry, he nursed in his mind a foolish disesteem of kings, and proclaims that 'he never sees courts.' Yet a little regard shown him by the Prince of Wales melted his obduracy; and he had not much to say when he was asked by his Royal Highness, 'How he could love a prince while he disliked kings.'"

Johnson's best poetry is the versified expression of the tone of sentiment with which we are already familiar. The *Vanity of Human Wishes* is, perhaps, the finest poem written since Pope's time and in Pope's manner, with the exception of Goldsmith's still finer performances.

o

Johnson, it need hardly be said, has not Goldsmith's
exquisite fineness of touch and delicacy of sentiment.   He
is often ponderous and verbose, and one feels that the
mode of expression is not that which is most congenial ;
and yet the vigour of thought makes itself felt through
rather clumsy modes of utterance.   Here is one of the
best passages, in which he illustrates the vanity of military glory :—

> On what foundation stands the warrior's pride,
> How just his hopes let Swedish Charles decide ;
> A frame of adamant, a soul of fire,
> No dangers fright him and no labours tire ;
> O'er love, o'er fear, extends his wide domain,
> Unconquer'd lord of pleasure and of pain ;
> No joys to him pacific sceptres yield,
> War sounds the trump, he rushes to the field ;
> Behold surrounding kings their powers combine,
> And one capitulate, and one resign :
> Peace courts his hand, but spreads her charms in vain.
> " Think nothing gain'd," he cries, " till nought remain ;
> On Moscow's walls till Gothic standards fly,
> And all be mine beneath the polar sky ?"
> The march begins in military state,
> And nations on his eye suspended wait ;
> Stern Famine guards the solitary coast,
> And Winter barricades the realms of Frost.
> He comes, nor want nor cold his course delay—
> Hide, blushing glory, hide Pultowa's day !
> The vanquish'd hero leaves his broken bands,
> And shows his miseries in distant lands ;
> Condemn'd a needy supplicant to wait,
> While ladies interpose and slaves debate
> But did not Chance at length her error mend ?
> Did no subverted empire mark his end ?
> Did rival monarchs give the fatal wound ?
> Or hostile millions press him to the ground ?
> His fall was destined to a barren strand,
> A petty fortress and a dubious hand ;

He left the name at which the world grew pale.
To point a moral and adorn a tale.

The concluding passage may also fitly conclude this survey of Johnson's writings. The sentiment is less gloomy than is usual, but it gives the answer which he would have given in his calmer moods to the perplexed riddle of life ; and, in some form or other, it is, perhaps, the best or the only answer that can be given :—

Conclusion

> Where, then, shall Hope and Fear their objects find ?
> Must dull suspense corrupt the stagnant mind ?
> Must helpless man, in ignorance sedate,
> Roll darkling down the torrent of his fate ?
> Must no dislike alarm, no wishes rise ?
> No cries invoke the mercies of the skies ?
> Inquirer cease ; petitions yet remain
> Which Heaven may hear, nor deem religion vain ;
> Still raise for good the supplicating voice,
> But leave to Heaven the measure and the choice
> Safe in His power whose eyes discern afar
> The secret ambush of a specious prayer.
> Implore His aid, in His decisions rest,
> Secure whate'er He gives—He gives the best.
> Yet when the scene of sacred presence fires,
> And strong devotion to the skies aspires,
> Pour forth thy fervours for a healthful mind,
> Obedient passions and a will resign'd ;
> For Love, which scarce collective men can fill ;
> For Patience, sovereign o'er transmuted ill ;
> For Faith, that panting for a happier seat,
> Counts Death kind nature's signal of retreat.
> These goods for man the laws of Heaven ordain,
> These goods He grants who grants the power to gain ;
> With these Celestial Wisdom calms the mind,
> And makes the happiness she does not find.

THE END.